THE ALCOHOLIC EMPLOYEE

Drug Abuse and Alcoholism Series

Major Modalities in the Treatment of Drug Abuse
Brill, L., M.S.S. and Lieberman, L., M.A., (eds.)
Methadone
Chambers, C.D., Ph.D. and Brill, L., M.S.S. (eds.)
The Alcoholic Employee
Brisolara, A., M. Ed.
The Alcoholisms
Jacobson, G.R., Ph.D.
Before Addiction
Lieberman, F., D.S.W., Caroff, Pi, D.S.W. and Gotlesfeld, M., M.S.S.
Barbiturates
Wesson, D.R., M.D. and Smith, D.E., M.D.

THE ALCOHOLIC EMPLOYEE

A Handbook of Useful Guidelines

by Ashton Brisolara, M.Ed.

Executive Director
Committee on Alcoholism and Drug Abuse
for Greater New Orleans

HUMAN SCIENCES PRESS
72 Fifth Avenue 3 Henrietta Street
NEW YORK, NY 10011 • LONDON, WC2E 8LU

Library of Congress Catalog Number 78-15763

ISBN: 0-87705-327-8

Printed in the United States of America
9 987654321

Library of Congress Cataloging in Publication Data

Brisolara, Ashton.
  The alcoholic employee.

  Includes index.
  1. Alcoholism and employment—Handbooks, manuals, ets. 2. Alcoholism—Handbooks, manuals, etc. 3. Alcoholism—Treatment—Handbooks, manuals, etc. I. Title.
HF5549.5.A4B74   658.38'2   78-15763
ISBN 0-87705-327-8

CONTENTS

PREFACE

It has been estimated that the loss due to excessive drinking on the part of people engaged in industry runs into billions per year. This is a staggering price to pay for an illness that is treatable and from which so many people recover. In spite of this, however, millions of people continue to suffer from this problem and industry continues to suffer the accompanying economic loss.

This handbook represents a definite aid to those interested in relieving this problem. It describes the ramifications of the problem and presents to the reader an overall picture of the excessive drinking in industry and what can be done about it. Written by one experienced in the field, who has studied the problem carefully, and who has reviewed the results of the implementation of the program recommended, it presents in concise form a method of approaching the problem with a view of saving industry billions of dollars.

For many years, alcoholism has been looked upon

as a moral problem, and its victims as moral derelicts. As a result of this, many competent individuals have been deprived of their employment because of what was thought to be a weak will or perverse willfulness. With greater understanding of the illness and the personality problems involved, alcoholism has come to be recognized as a treatable illness and one in which the patients respond to proper care as well as they do to any other chronic illness. With this in mind, enlightened industry has undertaken to accept its responsibilities in this matter and protect the tremendous investment it has in competent employees who have become ill. Management has been joined by enlightened labor unions in their efforts to solve this problem.

With proper treatment, such employees have been rehabilitated to their former competency, and recovered their physical and emotional health. They have resumed their work with as great an efficiency as they ever had. This has represented a tremendous saving in personnel investment and has proven to be an economic asset for industry.

This handbook provides for those who must cope with alcoholism and drug abuse, a method of approaching the problem in individual plants and with all employees. To follow these programs will undoubtedly prove beneficial to the employee and the employer as well.

MARVIN A. BLOCK, M.D.
Past President
Committee on Alcoholism
American Medical Association

Chapter 1

INDUSTRIAL ALCOHOLISM

Have you ever been faced with a problem employee, one whom you suspect is drinking too much, a skilled and experienced individual, long time "company man or woman," likable, willing, a potential winner, a friend who is going down the drain?

What can you do? What can you say? How can you say it? Even if you *can* and *do*, will it help? Are you the right person? Can you turn the tide of certain disaster? Suppose the employee denies he or she has any problem? What if he or she becomes resentful or hostile? Will he or she accept it if you say that alcoholism is the problem? Is that the right thing to do? The questions seem endless, their answers painful. Nonetheless, it is the normal, everyday dilemma faced by those in supervision, in management, and in authority. When the opportunity of redirecting the troubled employee is neglected, endless problems, crisis situations, loss of productivity, disciplinary actions, and eventually costly termination ensue.

Viewed objectively, employee management can be tracked practically as seen in Chart 1.

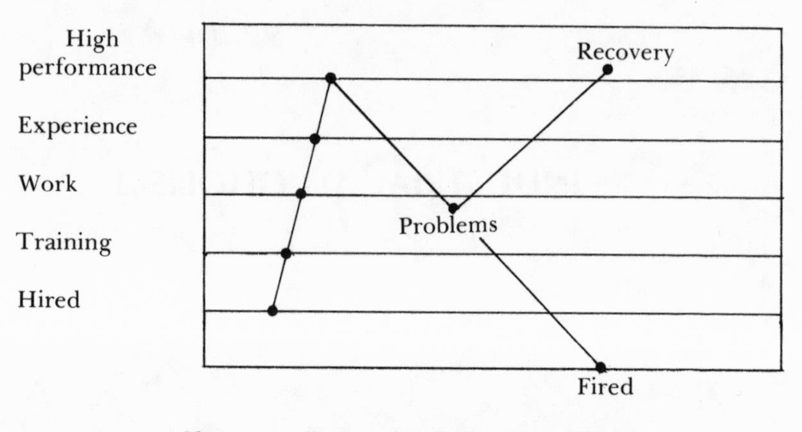

Chart 1. Occupational Employee Cycle

The company hires someone for a specific task.

A period of training, an investment in time and money, follows.

A trained employee is then placed in the work force.

In time, the employee becomes experienced, skilled, and productive.

Finally, the employee is established as an excellent performer.

For many such employees the story is one of rapid rise in company ranks, greater achievement, productivity, and higher income. But for some, destined to the same, the heavy clouds of problems arise and begin to engulf them, so that, in time, the productivity expected from an experienced and highly skilled individual begins to wane. It ultimately alters the worker to a problem—a problem to the supervisor, to the personnel department, and to the company.

It doesn't matter that the problem lies within the employee or elsewhere—at home with a husband or wife, a son, or a daughter—it begins to take a heavy toll on performance.

What should be done?

The choice is a very simple, although difficult, one. Either endeavor to guide and direct the employee to help, which, if accepted, will probably return him or her to high performance again, oftentimes even greater than formerly; or deny a problem exists or for whatever reason allow the problem to continue to grow, which will eventually culminate in disciplinary action and termination—costly and painful to both employer and employee.

It is for that reason that practical handling of such problems is important, no, it is imperative, to smooth business operations and profit.

Is There A Problem?

Alcohol problems? Alcoholism in my company? How can that be possible? We haven't had anyone arrested, jailed, or drunk on the street.

Perhaps it is difficult to admit that alcoholism has ever existed in your company, or that anyone you have seen go down the drain was really an alcoholic. You always figured that there must have been something else, something that you and the company did not see, did not comprehend. But alcoholism? That seems to be a hard pill to swallow.

"A management which says it has no problem drinkers doesn't know what it is talking about." So said Dr. J. L. Norris, Medical Director, Kodak Park Division, Eastman Kodak Company.[1]

In the past, the general attitude of industry has

been a complete and tenacious denial that alcoholism existed within its circle of influence. When it was encountered, it was interpreted for the most part as a disciplinary problem to be dealt with by either severe warnings or terminations. Today, there is a realization that the problem exists in any and all industrial and business complexes.

There are an estimated five (5) million alcoholics who are employed in our nation, according to the National Council on Alcoholism.

Conservative estimates point to an industrial alcoholism problem affecting five (5%) percent of any work force.

Alcoholism costs industry over 10. 4 billion dollars annually.

The average alcoholic is absent 22 more days per year because of his or her illness than the nonalcoholic, who is absent, according to statistics, from 6 to 10 days a year.

Most alcoholics have been employed by their company for an average of 10 years. They are usually experienced and key personnel, at their peak of productivity.

According to Oates, "There are direct costs, primarily resulting from lost manhours of work, from long periods of related disability, from medical and hospital expenses, and from the expense of replacing trained workers of all ranks."[2]

The indirect cost is impossible to calculate, but the scope of the problem is identified by H. David Archibald, Director of the Toronto Alcoholism Foundation, who said, "Double your best guess at the number of 'worrisome drinkers' in your company for the most likely estimate."

As Dana cleverly devised, a typical case would be John Smith, whose personnel record account might possibly read as follows:[3]

JOHN SMITH, 1975

ASSETS	*LIABILITIES*
Fully trained	Somewhat aggressive
Concientious	Could be neater in appearance
Works well with others	
Good health	
Low scrap rate	
Considered for advancement	
Rarely absent	
Efficient	
Alert	

As his diminishing value becomes apparent, his record, some time afterwards, might well read as follows:

JOHN SMITH, 1985

ASSETS	*LIABILITIES*
Fully trained	Very aggressive
	Slovenly appearance
	Efficiency down
	Scrap rate high
	Absent frequently
	Sometimes reports to work drunk
	High accident rate
	Does not work well with others
	Far from conscientious
	No advancement potential

Though John Smith's "profit and loss" analysis reveals a liability to his employer, many of the liability items could easily be eradicated by the elimination of the problem which is indicated by the symptoms. So the case is far from hopeless. Left untreated, however, his condition will worsen to the point that the only possible solution will be termination of employment.

The Important Decision

Which is it to be: *firing* or *helping*? Which is more essential? Which is more humane? Which is more economical?

John's 14 years of service can scarcely be easily replaced. His actual worth to the company may be difficult to evaluate and determine. His knowledge, experience and training could represent thousands of dollars of company investment. It would be wasteful to fire John without endeavoring to motivate him to seek help. Even if a comparable replacement could be found, it would probably cost the company another substantial investment to train the new employee, and the possibility arises that he might never reach John's capabilities, or possibly have or develop a similar problem. It is much more economical to offer John help, which, if accepted and successful, would return his personnel record account to a heavily lopsided asset for his employer.

As a human being, there is no possible price tag that can be placed on John. It goes beyond his own life to his wife, children, relatives, his future, and even the community that might be called on to bear the cost of health and possible welfare payments. Denied a reasonable chance to obtain treatment, this once-useful and productive individual could well be thrown on the overcrowded labor market, with no possibility, because of his age and circumstances of termination, of finding employment. He could well end up on skid row or welfare.

Handling alcoholism is not a "wishy-washy," "coddling" type of operation, whereby employees are given endless opportunities and chances. Industry is not a haven for misfits or a rehabilitation center. *Firmness* must permeate the entire process. Offered reasonable opportunities of accepting help, the employee who denies the problem and refuses treatment and even diagnosis, leaves his or her employer no choice. For the sake of the company, the safety of the work force, and for the actual benefit of the alcoholic, who, if left to progress will destroy himself or herself, the only solution is termination. When this is done, everyone is the loser: the company, production, and, at times, the alcoholic.

It may sound paradoxical to phrase that the alcoholic *might be the loser* in such termination cases. At times, termination is the means by which the alcoholic, faced with unemployment, is shaken into the reality of his or her plight and the need for seeking help. Termination can be a very powerful motivating factor. With some alcoholics, it takes years of geographic and job changes before the realization that help is needed becomes apparent. In this interim, everyone connected with the alcoholic suffers heartaches, inconveniences, disappointments, and financial losses.

Despite the effectiveness of the threat of termination in prompting motivation, this should be the last contemplated step in coping with the problem drinker.

THE HALF-MAN

Perhaps the most insidious employee is the alcoholic Henderson calls the "Half-Man." So called because though present at work, he gives his employer but half or less of his potentials.

Alcoholics can remain on the payroll for years with no apparent difficulty or sign of an alcohol-related problem. Arriving on time, they perform at half speed, either to avoid errors or because of the realization of diminished mental or physical dexterity. The loss of such productivity is enormous. Meanwhile, the illness progresses, always approaching the inevitable climax—termination.

Sam, the Half-Man in Industry, can be a craftsman, foreman, salesman, senior executive, or one of any fellow workers.[4]

The Answer

When faced with such striking evidence that alcoholism is an illness, that it does prevail in every business or industry, and has devastating toll on productivity, the only solution to the problem is to acknowledge its existence and take appropriate remedial and preventive action.

Over the years, progressive companies have taken the initiative and organized industrial alcoholism programs, now often called Employee Assistance Programs. Some of the pioneers in the field are Allis-Chalmers, Consolidated Edison, Bell Telephone of Canada, DuPont, American Cyanamid, Eastman Kodak, and Kemper Insurance, to name a few.

These companies initiated action whereby the problem of alcoholism was not only identified and recognized, but effectively handled. Furthermore, a program of prevention was initiated on a sustained basis.

Alcoholism was incorporated as a part of the educational policies of these companies and special emphasis was put on the medical department's role in both detection and treatment. Some have developed special employee medical charts that have reference to drinking and alcohol-related problems.

An industrial alcoholism program is simple. It consists of:

sam the puzzled man

1. *promotion*

After having been with the company for 15 years, Sam is chosen to head the "new model project." During the last five years Sam's drinking has increased, but this is not the sort of thing anyone would talk about, and, of course, it would not appear on any record.

2. *celebration*

To celebrate his good fortune, Sam drinks perhaps a little more than the rest of the boys, just as he has for years. One drink usually leads to another and another. His friends seem to be able to "take it or leave it." But, somehow, once Sam starts to drink, he finds it hard to stop. Drinking has become a real problem to him.

3. *monday absentee*

Sometimes Sam's "evening out" with the boys leads to heavy week-end drinking. The resulting hang-over makes him unable to report to work on Monday morning. Sam is absent more than twice as often as the average employee and draws three times as much in sickness payments.

4. *blackout*

After an evening of drinking, Sam is puzzled the next morning by a blackout — a temporary loss of memory. He can recall nothing that happened the night before. Back at work, Sam finds it difficult to make accurate calculations for the new model, but he has learned how to "cover up." Neither he nor his boss admits that Sam has any problem with drinking.

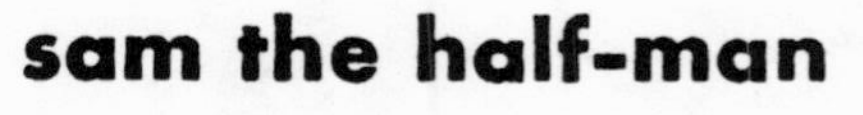

sam the half-man

5. *cover up*

"He's Sam the half-man," joked Tom one Tuesday. "Sam's body came to work, but his mind didn't come along. His work is all cockeyed." But good old Tom won't squawk. If he did the company would just fire Sam, fine him, or bawl him out. So Tom continues to cover Sam's absences and mistakes.

6. *late to work*

Sam finds that he needs an "eye opener" to help start the day. Being just a little late to work becomes a habit, but the company guard does not report Sam to management. This makes it easier for everyone to ignore the situation.

7. *alibi*

Sam develops lots of alibis for his drinking. Drinking becomes increasingly important to him. After all, his new job brings lots of responsibility; things aren't going well at home; bills are mounting up. Sam often has "one too many" after work, and Tom has to help him home.

8. *drink alone*

Sam begins to drink alone on week ends. His wife and children often go out to avoid unpleasant scenes with him. Sam drinks a lot and eats very little. He is nervous and has trouble sleeping. Frequent "colds" cause increasing absences from work, usually just after pay day.

sam the troubled man

9. *hidden problem*

Often Sam is shakey and nervous during the morning work hours, but a drink with his lunch "at the place across the street" makes him *feel* alert and much more steady although it actually dulls his brain and nerves. Sam covers this up. He is a half-man with a hidden problem.

10. *one of sam's days*

Occasionally Sam has days when he just sits at his work with his tools in approximately the usual order. His thoughts are rather vague and depressing. At times he thinks of the kind of a person he might have been. The little work that he does is filled with mistakes.

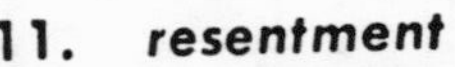

11. *resentment*

Sam shaves carelessly, and his general appearance becomes untidy. When fellow workers try to point out that he is drinking too much, Sam is resentful. Worry over the new model adds to his tension. Week-end drinking grows heavier. Mondays become increasingly difficult. Sam is a victim of alcoholism.

12. *the big test*

The new model is complete. To the company it represents thousands of dollars. To Sam it represents his big chance. But when test time arrives, Sam is not there. Instead of facing the tension of this crisis, he goes off on a real drinking bender.

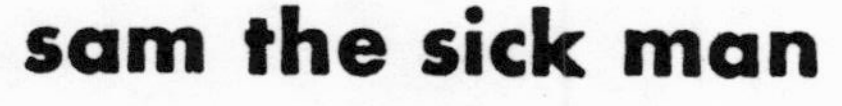

sam the sick man

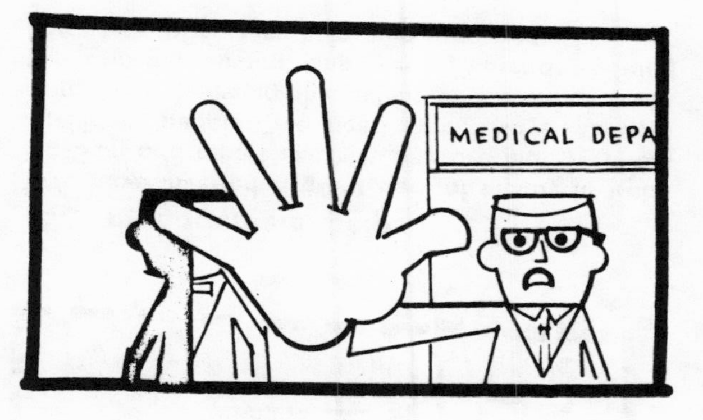

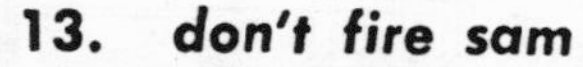

13. *don't fire sam*

"Stop," says the company medical director. "Alcoholism is an illness and a company health problem. We need to recognize that Sam is sick. Alcoholism can be successfully treated, especially in its early stages. Everyone should know the danger signs of alcoholism and the facilities offered for treatment."

14. *fellow workers help*

"By trying to cover up Sam's drinking problem, we have been unjust to him, his family and ourselves," say his fellow workers. "Instead of trying to hide Sam's trouble we should work with the medical department and help him to seek professional guidance and treatment. This calls for real teamwork by medicine, labor, and management."

15. *management helps*

"We have invested a great deal of money in training Sam and others like him who are highly skilled, intelligent people. We need them," says management after assessing the extent and costs of problem drinking among employees. "Instead of firing Sam, let's offer him help and treatment."

16. *company program*

With the help of the medical department, an educational and treatment program is organized at the company. A special supervisor is appointed to head the new program, which enlists the aid of all personnel at the plant and every available resource in the community to fight this illness.

sam the whole man

17. *special treatment*

Sam is treated by the company's medical department and is referred for additional help to the Committee on Alcoholism for Greater New Orleans who will refer him for treatment to the Clinic for the Diagnosis and Treatment of Alcoholism. So, Sam starts a treatment program which assists him in learning how to deal with his anxieties and to abandon alcohol as an escape from them.

18. *continued help*

To solidify these gains against an illness which has taken years to develop, Sam needs the support and understanding of his family, employer, Alcoholics Anonymous, clergy, clinic, and friends. With their assistance, Sam becomes a whole man again — an asset to his community and his company.

(Originally produced, developed, and prepared by the Connecticut Commission on Alcoholism, now the Alcohol & Drug Dependence Division of the Department of Mental Health, State of Connecticut, Hartford, Connecticut. Subsequently reproduced and published by the State of Michigan, Department of Public Health, Lansing, Michigan, and the State of North Carolina, Department of Human Resources, Division of Mental Health, Raleigh, N. C. Permission to reproduce from these agencies acknowledged, and credit given.)

1. *Management's acceptance* of the fact that alcoholism is an illness, to be treated as any other health problem.
2. *Supervisory staff meetings* to educate key personnel on alcohol, alcoholism, and detection techniques.
3. The organizing of a *referral system,* whereby detected problems can be adequately handled.

The Results

The results of such industrial alcoholism programs have bordered on the unbelievable. Here are a few remarks made by companies that have maintained ongoing alcoholism programs:

Allis-Chalmers:	"Absentee rate slashed from 8% to 3% and discharge rate from 95% to 8%. Savings to company of some $80,000 per year estimated."
Consolidated Edison:	"60% successfully rehabilitated. Absenteeism reduced from 14 days to 4 days per annum."
Great Northern Railway:	"We of course are well aware of the realistic benefits to us, safety-wise, and in terms of performance of duties, reliability, morale, public relations, etc."
Detroit Edison:	"Absenteeism reduced from twice company aver-

	age to one-half company average."
DuPont:	"950 alcoholics—1.09% of employees—66% successfully rehabilitated."
Minnesota Mining:	"80% are either recovered or controlled to the point where noticeable and marked improvement in attendance, productivity and family and community relationships now exist."
Peoples' Light and Coke Company:	"Program has been effective in 50%–60% involved."

In a report entitled "A Treatment Program for the Alcoholic in Industry," which appeared in the *Journal of the American Medical Association,* the following results were reported:[6]

> Experience with 180 alcoholics referred by 14 industrial organizations to an independent joint clinic for alcoholism showed that 135 were able to maintain a sufficient degree of control over their drinking to hold their jobs, and those who took treatment showed a reduction of absenteeism to one-third of the pretreatment figure.
>
> Of 23 alcoholics who were referred to the clinic but who refused treatment, 13 were able to retain their jobs. . . .

The fantastic recovery rate should come as no secret. Occupational problems are usually detected at an early stage in the development of the illness, and usually at a time when the individual is still securely employed, still united with his or her family, and at relatively comfortable financial status. Extending a helping hand coupled with the obvious elimination of the ill-founded stigma that has for so many years shrouded the illness, acceptance of alcoholism is more easily promoted, and because there is so much at stake to lose, motivation is more in earnest.

From a therapeutic standpoint, patients who are still employed and with their families have recovery rates of 70% and better. Those who are divorced or separated and unemployed have only an 8% recovery rate.

From a management standpoint, the dividends of approaching alcohol and drug problems in a realistic manner are many. There is a diminishing and, at times, elimination of crisis situations that can be so emotionally exasperating and time consuming; there is a practical extension of the company's health policies and services, which, in the past, have hidden illnesses such as alcoholism, allowing for recurrences and deterioration; there is usually an overall promotion of safety, respect for human dignity, and goodwill; it makes for a closer-knit industrial family, where members are concerned not only with productivity, but with each other's welfare as well; profits increase.

Everyone benefits from an occupational program aimed at helping the troubled employee. The company's profits increase, problems are lessened, productivity increases, and human lives, the only irreplaceable commodity on Earth, is salvaged.

Why Such A Difficult Task?

With all of the apparent benefits in approaching the problem employee with a drinking problem in a positive and effective manner, why is there such hesitancy in implementing such a program within a company?

To begin with, an occupational program is often considered a prohibition movement by some people in top management. Fearful that it is a step to promoting abstinence, and "taking drinks away" from those who imbibe, resistance develops.

The feeling that alcoholics are skid row bums, scarcely to be found within a home or business, prevents easy acceptance. The old attitudes about the problem drinker with all of their preconceived erroneous concepts prevail.

There is a reluctance among fellow managers, supervisors, and workers to take part in what might at first appear to be a form of witch hunt, and even more hesitancy in identifying and documenting cases of problem drinking or any other problem, for that matter.

At times resistance within a company comes from a top management executive, who has the problem himself or herself, and is most threatened by any troubled employee program that might eventually strike at the root of a problem that has been successfully hidden thus far.

Thus, in spite of all of the benefits of an occupational program, its implementation is often slow, difficult, and trying. Perhaps when alcoholism and drug abuse are understood in their correct perspectives, when the most important ingredient of the program is understood—to help everyone—the concept can be more easily appreciated and accepted.

Labor, too, has a stock in the program. It is a real contribution to the welfare of the worker, an added insurance of stability in employment, and a health benefit in its truest sense that will help both labor and management to safeguard the well-being of workers, to facilitate the handling of employee problems, and to increase the productivity and hence the appreciation of employees.

It is a joint effort in industrial productivity and humanitarism. There can be no disagreement in this area of concern. Everyone benefits from such a program. There is no hiding of productionless workers, no argument about the direction to take, and total agreement should disciplinary action or even termination become necessary; everyone knows the policy, knows the process, understands the helping hand that is extended, realizes that productivity is an essential ingredient of the work world, knows that any problem will be handled in a humanitarian manner and with understanding, and that the company and the union care.

Summary

The problem of alcoholism has not only been recognized by management, but by labor as well. The AFL-CIO Publication No. 52, published by the AFL-CIO Community Service activities, explores "What Every Worker Should Know About Alcoholism." It would seem incredible that any company could be so naive as to deny that problems do exist in the confines of its industrial complex. Geographic changes or terminations are no solutions at all. They only put off the inevitable or pass on problems to other companies.

Perhaps the most comforting thought that should permeate any literature on industrial alcoholism is that the alcoholic, although sick, is *treatable.* The alcoholic can be returned to normal living and productivity in order to be able to give his or her employer not only the normal expectancy of work capacity, but probably much more. Finally, the commencement of any industrial alcoholism program is really not such a gigantic step. It consists of utilizing the three areas of:

Management
Supervisory staff
Referal

References

1. Norris, J. L., M.D. *What to do about the employee with a drinking problem.* Chicago, Ill.: Kemper Insurance, p. 2.
2. Oates, James F., Jr. Address given at the Annual Meeting of N.C.A., New York City, March 28, 1958.
3. Dana, Allan H. *Alcoholism, a credit entry.* Avon Park, Fla: Florida Rehabilitation Program.
4. Sam the Half-Man. Developed, prepared, and produced by the Connecticut Commission on Alcoholism, now the Alcohol & Drug Dependence Division of the Department of Mental Health, State of Connecticut, Hartford, Connecticut. Subsequently reproduced and published by the State of Michigan, Department of Public Health, Lansing, Mich., and the State of North Carolina, Department of Human Resources, Division of Mental Health, Raleigh, N.C.
5. Rouse, Kenneth A. *What to do about the employee with a drinking problem.* Chicago, Ill.: Kemper Insurance, p. 3.
6. Pfeffer, Arnold A., M.D. Feldman, Daniel J., M.D., Feibel, Charlotte, Frank, John A., Cohen, Marilyn, B. A., Berger, Stanley, Ph.D., Fleetwood, M. Freile, M.D., Greenberg, Sidney S., M.D. A Treatment program for the alcoholic in industry. *Journal of American Medical Association*, June 30, 1956, 161, (9).

Chapter 2

ALCOHOL

History

Alcohol, a controversial and mysterious liquid, has been part of man's culture since the beginning of time. It is the common belief that alcohol was accidentally discovered by Noah, who, according to the Book of Genesis, left grape juice in the vineyard, which ultimately fermented into wine, resulting in his intoxication.

Regardless of when and where it was discovered, alcohol played an important part in the life of primitive peoples. It contributed, in no small way, to the feeling of tribal togetherness, and, despite the fact that it was surrounded with multitudinous mysteries, controls, and taboos, it became in many instances part of religious ritual. It remains as such today.

Over the years, alcohol has been consistently associated or identified with social problems. As a consequence, attitudes toward the beverage varied, often with little consideration for its users.

Probably because of significant abuses, history relates a number of classic stances taken on the subject. King Hammurabi, in 225 B.C., imposed a number of price-fixing and dispensing controls on alcoholic beverages. Gautama Buddha taught total abstinence to his followers, even though modern Buddhists have departed from this stand. The Greeks looked on alcohol as a sign of barbarism and viewed drunkenness as totally disgraceful. The Spartans, at one time, eliminated all drinking establishments. Despite the fact the Romans were drinkers, Emperor Domitian destroyed half of all the Roman Vineyards in 75 A.D. and forbade the planting of more. This law was repealed a few years later, and probably had been originally passed to insure against possible intoxication and rebellion. Mohammed, in the Koran, prohibited the use of all alcoholic beverages for his followers.

Early colonists in this country brought with them their European drinking habits. Most considered alcohol as a beverage and some as medicine. The New World made its contribution to the alcohol culture by the introduction of rum made from fermented cane juices and molasses.

America's drinking habits changed drastically during the frontier era. Intoxication rather than good fellowship prevailed, so that by the end of the sixteenth century Americans had already developed a reputation for being hard drinkers. The years that followed were marked by an expansion of distilling alcoholic beverages; by 1792 the annual consumption of hard liquor was estimated to be 2.5 gallons per person and 20 years later to be 4.7 gallons per person.

By the middle of the nineteenth century, America was ripe for drastic changes in its drinking laws. At first, pledges were sought for total abstinence; and finally, a group of individuals came to the conclusion that the only way to cope with the issue of drinking was by legislation. In 1920, Congress passed the Nineteenth Amendment to the Constitution, which prohibited the production of alcohol in the

United States. The 13 years that followed were filled with traumatic problems until the amendment was finally repealed.

The controversy continues, even today. There are those who feel that alcohol should be abolished to eliminate the problems that are associated with its abuse. Others feel that "For those who can, drinking can be fun," and should not be eliminated because of a minority of abusers and pathological drinkers.

WHY DO PEOPLE DRINK?

If someone wishes to drink, he or she needs no reason. There are probably as many reasons for drinking as there are drinkers. The fact remains that if one wishes to drink, he or she will do so, regardless of the reason.

Some claim they like the *taste* of alcohol. Actually alcohol is odorless, colorless, and tasteless. The various "tastes" of bourbon, rye, scotch, and so on, make certain beverages palatable to particular individuals. The peppermint taste of creme de menthe is not the alcohol, but the taste that has been inserted to give it its own peculiar taste or characteristic.

Others claim they drink to *have fun.* And perhaps there is some semblance of truth to this. To a point, drinking can be fun. Past a point, however, drinking can become painful. The individual who claimed that he had the best New Year's Eve party of his life, saying he was sick for 5 days, can scarcely admit that the experience was enjoyable. How can one say that feeling numb, not being able to speak, walk, and being sick for 5 days be associated with fun? One can have fun without drinking.

For some drinkers, alcohol is a *medium of toast.* One can always find something to toast. A baby is born, and we toast the new arrival with a drink. Someone passes away, and after the wake, everyone visits the tavern or lounge to toast the departed loved one, perhaps toasting one drink for every year he lived (which perhaps might have been 85 years!).

We drink in the summer *to keep cool;* in the winter, *to keep warm.* There is always a reason for drinking.

A small percentage of drinkers use alcohol as a *crutch,* to escape the pressures of life: their spouse, their work, their neighborhood, the noise of the children, themselves, and life itself. These are the type drinkers who eventually become involved in a drinking problem.

TYPES

While there are many types of alcohols, Americans come in contact with two almost daily. Methyl alcohol (wood or denatured alcohol) is used commercially; ethyl alcohol is the type consumed internally.

Alcohol is produced very simply through a process of fermentation. Grapes produce wine; grains produce beer or mash from which are made other types of alcoholic beverages; and molasses, rum.

Beer varies in strength from 3% to 8% alcohol by volume, with most beers being 4% to 6% in strength. A 12-ounce bottle of beer is equivalent in alcohol content to a 1-ounce highball.

Wines are usually 12% by volume, although there are some lesser in strength and others fortified that run as high as 23% by volume.

Champagne is carbonated wine. The only effect on absorption is that the carbonation allows alcohol to be taken into the body more readily.

Hard liquors or *spirits* are made by a process of distillation. This is an operation based on the fact that alcohol has a low boiling point and consequently, when the mash, wine, or fermented molasses are heated, the alcohol easily evaporates. When condensed or distilled, the beverage produced contains a higher percentage of alcohol.

Spirits are rated in strength by "proof," a term said to have originated in Kentucky where buyers wanted "proof" of the alcohol in the whiskey they bought. They poured a bit of the beverage in a saucer, sprinkled it with gun powder, and ignited it. The more readily it burned, the more "proof" that it was alcohol. If it did not burn, they refused to purchase it, realizing that the alcohol content was minimal.

One hundred proof beverage is 50% alcohol; 80 proof, 40%; and so on. The "proof" divided by 2 gives the percentage of actual alcohol in the contents of the beverage.

As a food, alcohol is incomplete. It has no proteins, carbohydrates, vitamins, minerals, or fat value. It is, however, extremely high in calories; a highball has 150 calories and cocktails have as much as 200 calories.

DEFINITION

Alcohol is a depressant drug. It is a chemical cousin to ether, and while it does act as a stimulant in fostering better circulation, it tranquilizes the brain and slows down reflexes and performance. Like certain other drugs, alcohol is addictive, with alcoholic withdrawal resembling narcotic withdrawal.

According to a statement made by a previous surgeon-general, "alcohol could not pass the present standards of the Food and Drug Administration." It is toxic and addictive.

WHAT HAPPENS WHEN ONE DRINKS

Alcohol is not digested. It is absorbed through the walls of the stomach and the intestines into the bloodstream and carried to the brain (see Diagrams A and B). The absence of food in the stomach will prompt a speeding up of the absorption process. Consequently, a good safety rule for social drinkers is to eat something before drinking.

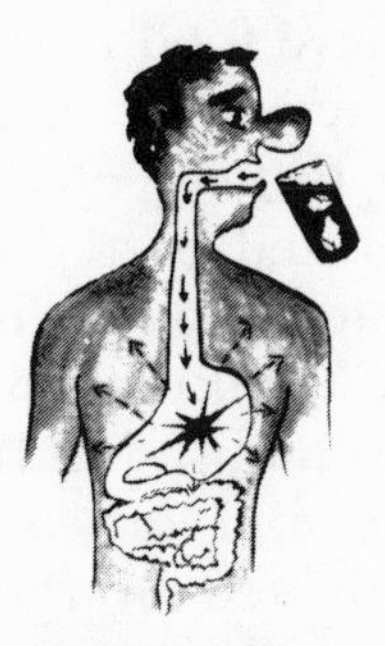

Diagram A Absorption Process

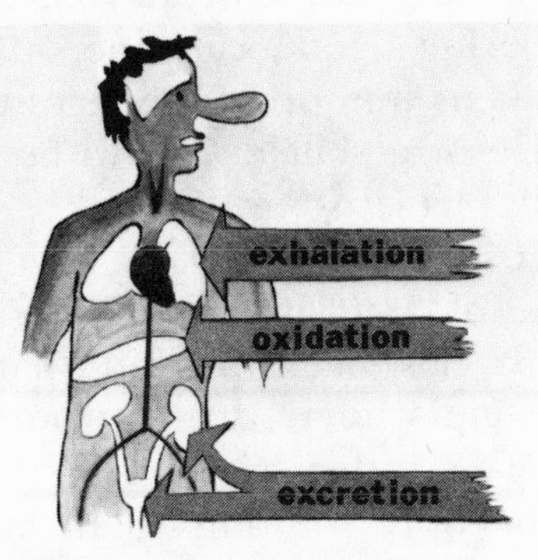

Diagram B Elimination Process

Young adults often suggest drinking a glass of cream before going to a party, so that the stomach will be coated and the capacity for alcohol enhanced. Others take a piece of butter or a spoonful of margarine to "grease the inside of their stomach" to be able to hold more alcohol. There are still those who feel that a glass of olive oil is the best way to ward off intoxication and increase capacity for alcohol.

There is no doubt that all of these techniques will slow down the absorption of alcohol. But so will potato chips, corn chips, popcorn, or any food whatever. The important thing is to have food in the stomach.

Alcohol is eliminated by exhalation, excretion, and oxidation. About 90% to 95% of the alcohol consumed internally must be oxidized by the liver. A healthy liver can oxidize approximately 1 ounce of alcohol per hour.

Actually one can drink a 1-ounce highball every hour on the hour for 6 months and never become intoxicated, because at the end of each hour the alcohol would have been eliminated by the action of the liver. Intoxication occurs when the alcohol gathers beyond the capabilities of the liver.

There is no quick way of sobering an individual who is intoxicated. Despite the custom that believes coffee to be a great sobering agent, caffeine only stimulates the drunk and awakens him or her to a condition that allows the performance of a skilled task without adequate control. You really have a "wide-awake drunk" on your hands in such a situation.

Finally, the old custom of walking a drunk is also quite useless. It has been proven that to appreciably sober up someone who is drunk would take 40 to 50 miles of walking—a rather awesome task.

Time is the only solution to inebriation, the only positive and assured sobering device. The best advice for someone who has imbibed too much is to go to bed and "sleep it off."

To understand the effects of alcohol on the user, let us assume that the drinker we will be considering weighs approximately 160 pounds, and that a drink is a 1-ounce highball or a 12-ounce bottle of beer. Factors affecting the speed of intoxication include weight, presence or absence of food in the stomach, rate of consumption, and tissue tolerance.

An individual who weighs 200 pounds can usually drink more than someone who weighs only 110 pounds. This is one reason that men usually drink more than women. Of course, there are exceptions. There are some very small and thin women who can outdrink two men who weigh over 200 pounds. The fluid in the larger person enables more alcohol to be consumed without its effects being felt.

If food is present in the stomach, the drinker will feel the effects more slowly than if the stomach is empty.

Naturally, the rate of consumption will affect the speed of intoxication. Nursing drinks will make intoxication less possible; gulping drinks will increase the chances of drunkenness.

Finally, individuals differ as to their tissue tolerance, or the body's ability to tolerate alcohol. Some have greater tolerance than others. Usually, ability to drink and to hold liquor increases with practice and with maturity but can be destroyed by abusive imbibing.

One or two drinks raises the blood level of alcohol approximately 0.02%. At this state of intoxication, the sensorium is influenced by the depression of the frontal lobe, affecting inhibitions and judgment (see Diagram C). Shyness is removed, fears are eliminated, and the individual is more inclined to say and do things that he or she would not normally say or do.

At this stage of intoxication, one can take advantage of the drinker. In a recent study it was found that a significant percentage of high school teenage pregnancies had a correlation with one or two drinks. A customer often responds to a sales pitch following a number of drinks. Others say embarrassing things, and workers have been known to lose their jobs by unwise comments

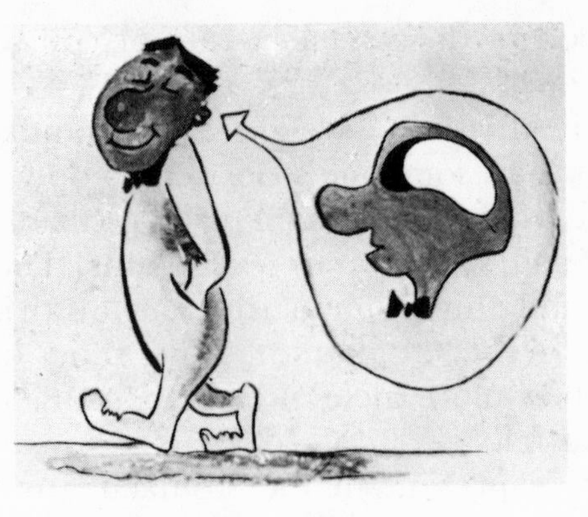

and remarks to their boss, all because their inhibitions had been removed by a few drinks.

Three or four drinks raise the blood level of alcohol to 0.06%. Because of the depression of the frontal and top center of the sensorium, reaction time and coordination are affected (see Diagram D).

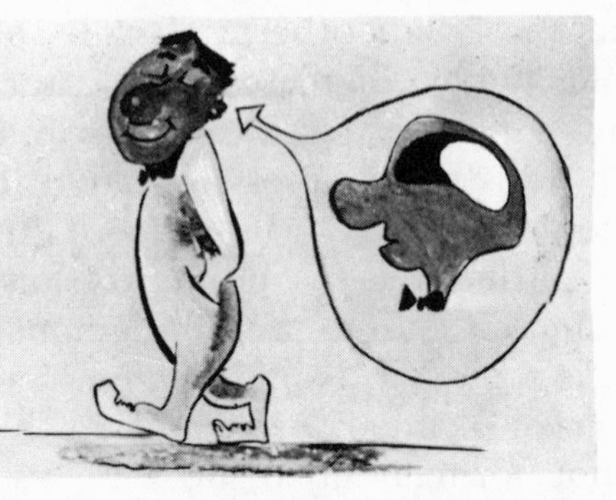

This is a stage of intoxication that prompts drivers to race up and down the highway, and teenagers to race down back roads at speeds beyond their capacity to handle. Moods have now changed, and the drinker risks life and limb if a skilled act is pursued.

Five or six drinks raise the blood level to 0.10%. This is legal intoxication in most states. At this stage of intoxication, vision, speech, and balance are noticeably affected. This precipitates a thick tongue, blurred vision, and contributes significantly to injuries, accidents, and fatalities (see Diagram E).

The driver at this stage is unable to see the stop sign, side road, or the pedestrian. Vision is blurred, reflexes are deadened. There is little semblance of reaction time and coordination. The drinker is a menace to himself or herself and others, should he or she endeavor to drive.

This stage of intoxication is the most dangerous. The drinker is "sober" enough to get into a car, drive, climb a ladder, operate a crane, or do some form of dangerous work, but "drunk" enough not to be able to perform such actions safely.

Eight, nine, or more drinks may raise the blood level of alcohol to 0.16%. Walking and standing are affected (see Diagram F).

Finally, when the blood level of alcohol reaches 0.40%, the anesthetic effect of alcohol becomes very apparent and the person is no longer in a vertical position but horizontal. He or she is then dead drunk and unconscious (see Diagram G).

Alcohol,—even the best,—can be poisonous if taken in large quantities. In such cases the portions of the brain which control breathing and heartbeat are depressed and the drinker dies of an overdose of alcohol in much the same manner as a barbiturate overdose. Drinking a fifth of whiskey, gin, vodka, or the like beverage if consumed and if not quickly regurgitated could cause such an overdose death.

The elimination of alcohol is a matter of mathematics. It takes about 1 hour for 1 drink to be oxidized, 4 hours for 3 drinks, 6 hours for 5 drinks, 10 hours for 8 drinks, and 26 hours for about 20 drinks.

Frequently, individuals who consume too much alcohol suffer a hangover. There is very little an individual can do to treat such a condition except sleep and rest. It is the price of abuse (see Diagram H).

The artist's concept of a hangover identifies the headaches, the effects of noise on the eardrums, the

feeling of dehydration, and the bloodshot eyes that often mark the "day after the night before."

As one begins to drink, he or she develops a tissue tolerance for alcohol. The person is able to hold more and more until a peak of tolerance is reached (Chart 2.1).

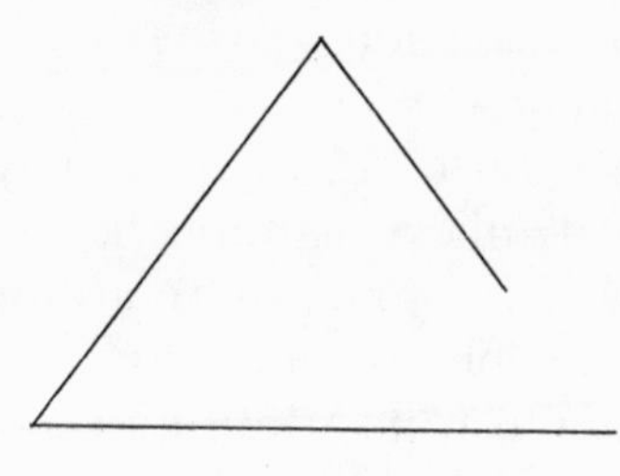

Chart 2.1 Tissue Tolerance

At that point, because of sickness, age, or some other condition, the drinker is unable to tolerate alcohol as before. Very heavy alcoholic drinkers frequently reach a peak of tolerance much earlier in life than moderate social drinkers, which is the price they pay for abusive drinking.

ALCOHOLISM

Alcoholism is not a matter of quantity or frequency of consumption. Some drinkers imbibe daily, and exhibit no problem; others drink seldom, but when they do, all sorts of difficulties arise.

There is no such thing as being a "little alcoholic." One is either alcoholic or not.

Alcoholism is best described as a progressive illness, marked by uncontrolled drinking that adversely affects one or more departments of life. Consequently, if drinking adversely affects social, economic, mental, emotional, physical, or spiritual life, this can be termed alcoholic or problem drinking.

The etiology of alcoholism has been a matter for discussion for years. There are many theories. Within the past 6 months, several scientists have claimed to identify the chemical in the alcoholic's body that makes him or her incapable of drinking socially and controllably. This confirms the long suspected physical component of alcoholism.

Only 7%, or 1 out of 15 drinkers, eventually become alcoholic. Some drinkers cannot become so involved, even if they tried. Of course, there are other factors that contribute to the problem, which are nonphysical.

Because alcoholism has definite social, mental, emotional, and spiritual ramifications, regardless of the etiology of alcoholism, perhaps the best approach to treatment is to take into consideration a human's total composition—body, mind, and soul—and involve all areas of life in treatment.

Unless treatment is initiated, alcoholism will continue to progress and will destroy its victim and his or her environment.

SIGNS OF ALCOHOLISM

Until such time that more sophisticated testing devices are developed, such as a physiological test, alcoholism can best be identified through some of the developing symptoms and behavioral expressions, such as:

Gross drinking behavior	—drinking more frequently and getting intoxicated more frequently than normal drinkers
Alcoholic blackouts	—suffering periods of amnesia following drinking
Loss of control	—inability to stop drinking once it is begun
Marital relationships affected	—family life and marital life adversely affected by drinking
Health affected	—overweight, underweight, liver problems, malnutrition, or anything that has been adversely affected because of alcohol consumption
Emotional involvement	—problems that arise because of excessive drinking
Financial problems	—loss of income, loss of money, waste, and financial difficulties attributed to excessive intake of alcohol

Crutch drinking	—drinking to solve problems, to face one's spouse, to make a sale, to meet the problems of everyday life, etc.
Alcohol-involved life	—alcohol surrounding and permeating life activity, such as eating, visits of friends, participation in social activities, etc.
Withdrawal	—"butterflies," shaky hands, hallucinations, convulsions, etc., when one is unable to obtain a drink following long binges
Employment problems	—losing time from work, tardiness, absenteeism, slow productivity, etc., because of alcohol
Spiritual problems	—not obtaining spiritual satisfaction from church because of a hangover, or giving up church altogether
Absenteeism	—invading workday and work schedule
Binges	—going on 2- and 3-day, 1- and 2-week sprees during which time drunkenness is maintained, and all else suffers

Loss of friends —not being invited to parties, friends avoiding you because of excessive drinking

Loss of hobbies —giving up sports, activities, and hobbies, because alcohol is not served at the location, or because alcohol has taken over

Denial —denying the fact that a problem exists, always ready with an excuse for one's drinking, always finding someone else whose drinking is worse in order to rationalize one's own drinking

Escape —drinking to escape one's surroundings, job environment, and self

Drinking when depressed —instead of seeking advice, looking for the quick and easy way out of depression and problems

Problem solving by drinking —avoiding the issue, and numbing oneself instead of seeking a solution to a problem

Morning drink —to get over the hump, to clear the "cobwebs"

Drinking obsession —being overconcerned

and over obsessed by drinking—when can I get the next drink? Whom can I visit who drinks? At this stage one drinks to live and lives to drink

Dependence on alcohol —being unable to live without alcohol

Hangovers —feeling horrible the day after drinking, headaches, upset stomach, etc.

Loss of job —because of drinking, even though it may have been identified as poor performance

Regardless of the specific sign or signs, any adverse condition brought about by abusive drinking is sufficient indication that a problem exists and an adequate reason exists to seek advice and help.

Although reluctant to accept it, the alcoholic actually realizes that something is amiss. Perhaps it is the shame of having to admit that a small object like alcohol has taken over command, or that the ill-founded stigma that has shrouded alcoholism for centuries prevents acceptance of the problem. Regardless, alcohol takes over, and, as the Japanese proverb so aptly puts it, "A man takes a drink; a drink takes a drink; and the drink takes man." When the man takes a drink, that's one thing. When the drink takes the man, that's alcoholism!

SOCIAL RAMIFICATIONS OF ALCOHOLISM

As alcoholism develops, one by one the various departments of life that help to promote and sustain a well-adjusted existence begin to deteriorate. The alcoholic may give up church, or at best continue attendance, but in such a hung-over condition that he or she receives no spiritual satisfaction. Church begins to bother the person's conscience, and so it is eliminated. Hobbies are also placed aside in lieu of alcohol. Activities of every type must surround the drinking experience, and hence hobbies become few and often nil. Friends, embarrassed and exasperated by the conduct of the alcoholic, eliminates him or her from invitations. It is frustrating to have to "deliver the drunken alcoholic home," or place him or her in a taxi with a tag for delivery. The easiest thing to do is to stop extending invitations, and that is exactly what occurs. Hopes and goals wane, until the only objective in the alcoholic's life is *alcohol.*

The family, the closest and most intimate part of the alcoholic's life, suffers too. The problem drinker consistently exhibits resentfulness and hostility to the ones he or she loves the most. The family ends up "on the rocks," to use a drinking expression. Love diminishes and is finally extinguished. All of the satisfaction that family life should bring is destroyed by drinking and the misunderstanding it fosters. Perhaps this is the most tragic consequence of alcoholism. It is a veritable hell-on-earth existence that destroys everything wholesome and good. Separation and divorce often follow.

Money soon becomes scarce, as it is wasted on excessive consumption of alcohol, in bizarre demonstration of generosity, or in drying-out periods in the hospital, where for most part the patient is "built up for the next drunk," under a multitude of diagnoses.

Finally, if nothing intervenes, the alcoholic begins to

exhibit resentfulness to his or her employer, goes on binges, and is finally terminated from employment. This individual is now at rock-bottom alcoholism, with nothing to hold him or her together, with nothing supportive left to lean on. At this point, some alcoholics commit suicide. It is the end of the trail.

When rock-bottom alcoholism has been attained, and it is inevitable unless death or treatment intervenes, even if treatment is introduced, recovery becomes more difficult, for the alcoholic will have nothing to return to, even if sober. Statistics bear out the point, as has been mentioned, that, if the alcoholic is still employed and still possesses his or her family, total recovery is more easily attained.

Physical Complications

Alcohol is a very toxic substance. Its abuse causes devastating physical deterioration. Unfortunately, alcoholism does not begin with pain, fever, or a sign of external infection. It nurtures itself on mental, emotional, social, and spiritual ills, insidiously invading every phase of life. Allowed to continue, unless death by accident occurs, the alcoholic will experience some of the painful side effects of alcohol's toxicity.

Among the most common forms of physical complications which are associated with alcoholism are:

Fatty liver
Cirrhosis of the liver
Abscesses of the lung
Pneumonia
Tuberculosis
Gastric problems

Heartburn
Ulcers
Perforated ulcers
Cancer of the throat
Primary cancer of the liver
Addiction and withdrawal
Delirium Tremens (DT's)
Pancreatitis
High blood pressure
Malnutrition
Overweight and underweight
Skin lesions
Change in hormone system
Brain damage

While most of the physical damage can be effectively treated by medication, appropriate diet, and abstinence, brain damage is irreversible, for brain cells cannot reproduce themselves. Whatever condition is precipitated is permanent and untreatable. It is a costly price for abuse.

TREATMENT

Unlike other illnesses, alcoholics cannot be catalogued into groups or types. Every problem drinker is different. As one psychiatrist put it so well, "Alcoholics are like everyone else, only more so." Each is different; each brings to treatment his or her own peculiar personality and characteristics, which must be taken into consideration before a plan of action or treatment is formulated and pursued.

Depending on the progressiveness of the illness and

the deterioration (physical, mental, social, spiritual, etc.) it has caused, a plan of treatment to meet the needs of the problem drinker must be laid out. There are a host of modalities of treatment and techniques for coping with the problem drinker. They include:

Individual therapy
Group therapy
Drug therapy
Antabuse
Transcendental meditation
Behavioral modification
Psychoanalysis
Outpatient treatment
Inpatient treatment
Alcoholics Anonymous
Hypnosis
Biofeedback
Religious conversation
Family therapy
Marriage and family counseling
Long-term inpatient treatment

Alcoholics do exhibit certain personality traits, but there is no unique alcoholic personality. Consequently, what works for one may be totally unsuccessful for another. Problem drinkers, we repeat, must be considered as individuals, with individual differences and needs, requiring different approaches to sobriety and rehabilitation.

Abstinence from alcohol alone is not synonymous with success. Rehabilitation means much more. It implies rebuilding the total person plus a degree of productivity, comfortableness with life, and happiness.

Industry, while relying on the expertise of the field and the modalities of treatment available, must direct its approaches to treatment acceptance in the area of work and productivity. Its approach is basically nontherapeutic, based on performance—the vital commodity of any business or industry.

Recovery

The most positive aspect of alcoholism is that problem drinkers do recover. Once denial is overcome and acceptance of one's inability to control alcohol permeates thinking, then the symptoms that have manifested themselves can be reviewed and corrected. This is the most important phase of the recovery program—surrender to the fact that alcoholism exists, that one is powerless over alcohol, that abstinence is necessary to commence the rehabilitation process, and that one cannot do it alone.

We suggest a dual approach to the problem. If we really believe what the field has been preaching, "that alcoholism is an illness," then we should direct or refer the alcoholic to a clinic, where professional diagnosis and assistance are available. The medical, psychological, social, and emotional aspects of the problem can best be handled by the professional, who can utilize in-depth techniques to overcome the damage that has occurred because of long-standing alcoholism.

We also suggest the utilization of Alcoholics Anonymous (AA), the fellowship of men and women who have a common problem—they are all alcoholics—and who support each other in their sobriety through a 12-step program of recovery. For many, this is all that is needed; for others, professional assistance is mandatory; for most, both are very useful. Within the fellowship, the alcoholic will find others who have had the same problem, who have gone the route of alcoholism in the identical manner, and who by a simple program of day-by-day sobriety, have attained weeks, months, and years of sobriety.

SUMMARY

Alcohol is our nation's most abused drug. The average age of alcoholics is now 25 to 30, as compared to the 1960 figure of 55 to 60. Younger and younger alcoholics are coming to the attention of health centers, and the probability exists that alcohol will replace, as it is actually doing at present, many of the other abused drugs in our society today.

According to latest statistics, about 90% of 17 to 19 year olds consume alcohol on a regular basis. The trend has been fostered probably because our society is more tolerant of alcohol consumption; it is legal, at least at certain age levels; it is used by two-thirds of our population; it is easily accessible. Again, our ultraliberal attitude to personal freedom and the cultural background of America's attitude concerning alcohol prompts more easily acceptance of the drug among young people.

One of every 15 drinkers will eventually become involved in a drinking problem. That 1 alcoholic will directly affect 4 other human beings, and indirectly 16 others. When one considers that there are a conservative 9.5 million alcoholics, the impact of the problem becomes more evident.

There is one fortunate facet of the problem: alcoholism is treatable.

The causes of alcoholism are many. There is a general agreement that a physical condition exists that makes it possible for some individuals to become alcoholic and others, not. There are accompanying psychological, environmental, and cultural aspects. Because the problem can trace its source in many directions, the approach to the alcoholic should be taken from the viewpoint of the total person—body, mind, and soul.

Chapter 3

Drugs

History

Use and abuse of drugs is not unique to the twentieth century. It is known that the Stone Age peoples had access to opium, hashish, cocaine, and probably other drugs.

In primitive religious rites, a variety of drugs were used. Evidently, the effect of drugs on its user awed the witnesses, and some misidentification with the deity resulted from the visible aftereffects. Warriors were oftentimes prepared for battle by the use of hashish or marihuana, and it is certain that available drugs were used to obtain a feeling of intoxication or euphoria, in addition to other more conventional uses.

The Chinese, long before the coming of Christ, used marihuana. Medically, it was administered for the treatment of gout, constipation, and even absentmindedness. Many other cultures were notorious for the use of marihuana for similar purposes.

Opium, which is derived from the poppy, has been used from earliest times. Before the Christian era, there were records of its use by the Egyptians, the Greeks, and the Romans, three of the outstanding civilizations of their times. It was primarily used by these cultures to induce sleep and relieve pain. As medical science developed and by the time of the Christian era, it was administered medically for the relief of cough, respiratory ailments, diarrhea, and insomnia. During the Renaissance period, when there was a great deal of interest in mental problems, opium was used for the treatment of hysteria. Amidst all of these medically oriented uses of drugs, the people of this era also used opium in attempting to dispel anxiety, boredom, despair, and reality.

By the eighteenth century, opium had found its way into American colonies where it was used to treat venereal disease, cancer, dysentery, menstrual pains, the pains of childbirth, and typhus fever. Later in the century, it was recognized medication in military hospitals. As its effectiveness grew, opiates were used for the treatment of all types of pain, including toothache and stomach cramps. However, little notice was given to the addictive qualities of the drug.

During the 1800s, the discovery of morphine and codeine began to alter the drug scene. At first, morphine was used to cure the opium habit, but because of the potency, it became very popular with opium users. In 1843, the hypodermic needle was invented, and through this means morphine was administered to Civil War soldiers who had been wounded in battle or who suffered from a variety of illnesses and diseases. By 1890, there was such a noticeable morphine problem, particularly among ex-soldiers, that it was tagged the "soldier's illness." Despite its medical use, morphine addiction was growing at such a pace that scientists began to search for a "cure." In the late 1890s, heroin was synthesized and used to treat morphine addicts.

As might be expected, it was not long before heroin became a problem. At first, the public disregarded the situation, disassociating the problem from the opium smokers who had been identified with the criminal element of our society. But this soon changed, as medical experts noted with dismay the growing addiction scene. Soon a conflict developed between the philosophy of "sickness" versus "crime." To some degree this conflict still exists.

The federal government first endeavored to control opium by prohibiting, except for medical purposes, the importing of opium and its derivatives. Addicts and users soon found ways of extracting the substances they s ught from medications on the market. In addition, an illegal flow of drugs developed.

In 1914, Congress passed the Harrison Act, which was aimed at regulation of all narcotic drugs. Laws governing the dispensing of such drugs, licenses, and other controls such as prescription requirements were introduced.

Pressure was soon exerted on the federal government to close down clinics that were dispensing habit-forming drugs to addicts on a maintenance basis. But this did not eliminate the problem as the black market grew and crime increased. Finally, law enforcement was brought into the area to curb the traffic and track down illegal users and distributors.

By 1930, the heroin problem had reached gigantic proportions. The government opened two hospitals for the treatment of heroin addiction at Lexington, Kentucky, and Fort Worth, Texas. Success was difficult, and the seriousness of the addiction was realized more fully.

After World War II, there was an increase in drug abuse and drug addiction. There had been exposure to drugs during the war in the Far East, and by the time the Vietnam war ended, many soldiers returned home from the war front addicted. In addition, the affluence of our society, the pressure that mounted during the 1960s, and general decay of law, order, and discipline, all contributed to an epidemic increase of drug abuse. It became the "in thing" and the fad of the day.

The country witnessed the "flower children," the "hippies," the growth of the "communes," and other bizarre drug related activity. Overdose death occurred more frequently, and the drug problem invaded the suburbs and middle-class Americans.

In recent years the federal government, as well as state and local governments, have reviewed and reshaped their drug laws. While there is general agreement on the majority of the controlling regulations, one specific area is under heavy fire—that is, the laws governing marihuana. Even though sentences have been reduced for the use and possession of the substance, there are those who believe it should be legalized in the same fashion as alcohol.

Causes Of Drug Abuse

It is not simple to pinpoint the causes of drug abuse. It is inconceivable to many why someone with access to the potentials that our civilization and culture offer would risk so much by taking illegal drugs or abusing legal ones.

One concept traces drug addiction to the *physical predisposition or condition* that craves sedation or out-of-the-normal feeling. This craving, once pampered, mentally develops into a habit that with increasing dosages, leads to physical addiction. Psychiatrically, some believe there exists a personality more prone to addiction than the normal being.

Recently, a theory has been expounded linking addiction to a specific area or lobe of the sensorium.

Sociologists place great emphasis on the *environ-*

ment as a leading cause of drug addiction in the United States. They point to the ghetto with its fatherless families, high unemployment, inadequate nutrition, poor medical services, improper educational facilities, high poverty level, and the existence of despair as contributing directly to the spread of heroin addiction. There is no doubt that addiction flourishes in the area of these socioeconomic conditions, but there is some question as to whether addiction would be totally eliminated should these problems be alleviated.

Some physiologists point to the use of drugs for the *relief* of pain, insomnia, tension, and exhaustion as the beginning of drug use. Such actions, coupled with continued use, terminates in addiction.

Certainly some proportion of abusers and drug addicts can trace their problem to the inordinate *desire for thrills.* Drugs appear to be most attractive when one has experienced the majority of normal, natural pleasures.

Boredom, rebellion, and *hostility* can play a role in the development of this problem. Commencing as an expression of one's feeling, it grows with the ultimate formation of addiction.

Peer pressures cannot be overemphasized in the drug culture. Because of an almost insatiable desire to be accepted and to be part of the "action," young adults are often misled and take drugs with ensuing risks. While there are many so-called "pushers" in America, the most numerous are peer distributors who give or sell to their friends.

One of the contributing causes is no doubt the *availability of too much legal and illegal* drugs in our society. Were drugs not so accessible, there would be a lessening of their abuse and addiction—though there would probably be some other type of problem that would be increased or precipitated.

In general, a human being endeavors to remain in tune or comfortable with life. Amid the extreme fluctuation of moods and feelings that range from the height of giddiness to the depths of despair, most people feel comfortable the majority of the time. They have no need for chemicals to improve their disposition or mental attitude. There are some, however, wallowing in an atmosphere of depression and despondency, who find immediate relief from their difficulties or hangups in drugs. There is no doubt that drugs will alter feelings. The problem, however, is that once metabolized, the problems return and there soon arises another problem—drug abuse or addiction.

Addiction Versus Habituation

Drug abuse terminology centers on dependency. Basically, however, all drugs fall under the category of *addictive* or *nonaddictive.* While the end result may be identical, there is an academic and practical difference.

An *addictive* drug creates a physical *dependency,* exhibits a *marked increase in tissue tolerance,* which is noticed by increased dosages, and *withdrawal* when addiction is reached and the drug is unavailable. Alcohol and heroin belong to this type.

Habituating or *nonaddictive* drugs are those that *do not create a physical dependency,* even though (in certain individuals) it may create a psychological dependence. There is *no increase in tissue tolerance* and *no physical withdrawal* involved when the drug is unavailable to the constant user. Such a drug is marihuana.

Philosophy

One of the best slogans that describes a healthy view of drugs in general is the inscription that appear on the door of the temple of Apollo in Greece. The inscription reads *Meden-Agan—Nothing in Excess.* Legal drugs do cause a gigantic problem in our country. They are often prescribed in excess and, more frequently, used in excess.

During the last few decades Americans have witnessed the development of drugs that have extended the average life span to 74 years. The sulphur drugs, penicillin, and antibiotics have enabled us to cure diseases that previously were deadly. One can scarcely identify evil with such use. The same wonder drugs, however, if abused or misused, can cause untold physical and psychological harm, and the use of illegal drugs or the use of legal drugs in an illegal manner can not only hurt the user physically and psychologically, but can also involve him or her with the law.

CLASSIFICATION

Drugs are divided into three types: *stimulants, depressants,* and *hallucinogens.*

Depressants tranquilize, depress, sedate, or slow down. They include all of the so-called "downers" and tranquilizers. They are countless in number.

Heroin—which is nicknamed horse, or H—is diacetyl morphine. It is derived from morphine and its effect is to depress the central nervous system.

The source of heroin, as well as all opiates, is the poppy plant. Heroin is much more potent than morphine. It resembles sugar and is distributed in large quantities called bundles and in single dosages called "papers." The pusher continually cuts the heroin in order to make additional profits. When heroin enters the country it can be 35 to 45% pure, but by the time it reaches certain sections of the United States, it can be as low as 3 to 12% pure heroin. It can be cut with sugar or flour, while brown sugar is commonly used in certain Latin American countries and in Mexico.

The user takes the powder, dissolves it in some type of solution. He or she draws the liquid into a hypodermic needle or a homemade eyedropper apparatus to which is attached a needle. A tourniquet is placed on the arm and the needle is injected into the vein. This is called *mainlining*.

Regardless of the effects or thrills that the potential addict obtains in the first shootings, when addiction is attained, the only satisfaction is the alleviation of withdrawal pains.

A synthetic narcotic called *methadone* is used in the treatment of heroin. It replaces heroin, serves in some cases as a blocking agent, and allows the addict to become more functional. Methadone is highly addictive and very difficult to detox. At best, it is only an interim approach awaiting a more permanent solution.

A *heroin user* usually exhibits pinpointed pupils following injection. The use of sunglasses to avoid detection of the pinpointed pupils is very common. Track marks or discoloration of the arms or other parts of the body resemble tattoos, occurring because of continued injection. To hide the marks, addicts often use long sleeves, even in the summertime. Following injection, addicts usually itch and begin to scratch. In later stages, there may be marked physical evidence of deterioration and other signs that only a physician could detect.

When an addict withdraws, he or she usually becomes nervous and shaky. Beads of perspiration will develop on top of his or her nostrils and he or she will exhibit a runny nose resembling a touch of hayfever. Finally, a pit of nausea will develop at which time the addict will be compelled to "shoot."

Alcohol is also a very commonly used depressant, with some alcoholics eventually becoming addicted to the substance. Alcoholics who are addicted, like other drug users, exhibit signs that have already been identified. Withdrawal includes tremors, shakes, convulsions, and visual and audio hallucinations, with extreme withdrawal or delirium tremens (D.T.'s) including lack of orientation, shock, and possible death.

Barbiturates, often called "goofballs" by abusers, are commonly misued by Americans. In fact, outside of alcohol, they are the most abused drugs in our society. Among the most common are seconal and phenobarbital. Barbiturates are both habit forming and addictive, with addiction most difficult to overcome, and withdrawal very dangerous.

In the balance of "good and evil," barbiturates have a varying effect depending on the use. It is prescribed for the control of epilepsy, the alleviation of insomnia, control of hypertension, and for relieving anxiety. Its abuse is followed by intoxication, constant use, addiction, overdose, and death. Obviously here is a perfect example of *Meden-Agan* with use being beneficial and abuse being very dangerous and destructive.

An abuser of barbiturates can usually be detected by an appearance of intoxication, accompanied by slurred speech, dilated pupils, clumsiness, stumbling, and in general, a "drunk" look without imbibing of alcohol.

Withdrawal from barbiturates is extremely dangerous and painful. It is accompanied by complete blackout, convulsions and shakes, and is sometimes fatal.

One of the most deadly of mixtures is alcohol and barbiturates. This combination has been the cause of countless deaths. In general, avoidance of drinking when medications are taken is a very good rule for conserving health.

Stimulants are drugs that (as the word describes) stimulate, excite, quicken, and speed. The most commonly used stimulants in the United States are amphetamines. College students often use Dexadrine and Benzedrine to stay awake in order to cram for examinations. Women are often amphetamine users in order to control or lose weight, since its use lessens the desire to eat and quickens activities that burn off excess calories.

Once the user becomes accustomed to various types of stimulants, the effect begins to wear off and the user must graduate to something more potent. In many cases, such abusers begin to use *methamphetamine* or *"speed."*

The use of such substances can be extremely dangerous. It makes the user very nervous and irritable and can cause visual distortions and physical shakes. Perhaps one of the most dangerous results in desiring to "come down" after an excessive use of such drugs is the use of depressants in order to make a "soft landing."

One of the drugs that is fast becoming a national epidemic is *cocaine.* Known as coke, C, snow, snowbirds, and so on, it is derived from coca leaves. Its chemical name is methylester or benzolecognonine. It can be injected, sniffed, or swallowed, and its effect is one of excitation. Users exhibit much the same effects as users of other stimulants.

A person who is abusing stimulants can usually best be detected by a hypermotor activity pattern, excessive nervousness, irritability, a loss of appetite, insomnia, and other physical conditions indicating over excitability. One of the dangers is that stimulants speed the body's functions, and like a machine, when the processes and mechanical parts are accelerated, a weakness is apt to develop.

LSD or "acid" as it is called is one of the most potent of the *hallucinogenic drugs.* It is actually becoming less popular because the toxic effect has been noticed even by those who claim to be clienteles of the drug culture.

LSD was commonly placed on sugar cubes and called by the term of "drop acid." The abusers today use it in liquids, or solids, and almost every other type of material that is edible is combined with it.

The experience that is derived by the LSD user and other hallucinogens takers is called a "trip." Trips that are pleasurable, giving hallucinations of an enjoyable nature are called *good trips.* Those that create a frightening or painful experience are called bad trips or *"bummers."* One is not assured of the type of experience that will be derived on the use of LSD.

A person on a LSD trip would probably exhibit erratic behavior, extreme apprehension, and hallucinations and, of course, if psychotic, could become quite dangerous and violent. Excessive use can cause brain damage and other toxic effects. One of the strangest phenomena connected with this drug is the "flashback," which occurs following the use of this drug. A trip may be precipitated without actually administering the drug. There have been some experts who claim that the flashback is nonexistent, occurring only because of the desire of the abuser to experience another trip sensation. Be that as it may, there are countless documented cases of flashbacks.

One of the dangerous effects of LSD is its use by the psychotic person. Often, a psychotic episode can occur, during which the individual might hurt himself or someone else. There is no way of determining which might occur.

Mescaline is another commonly used hallucinogen, which takes the place of LSD. Youthful abusers seek out this drug, which is derived from the peyote cactus. LSD is often sold on the street as mescaline.

Also included on the list of hallucinogenic drugs are the volatile substances such as glue, which, when inhaled from a plastic bag, often results in suffocation or damage to the liver or other organs. Teflon, which has been known to suffocate its victim; gasoline, which fortunately is not too frequently used because of its flammable qualities; and certian types of other volatile substances such as sprays and thinners are used to obtain the desired effect.

The most frequently used and abused drug, with the exception of alcohol and barbiturates, is *marihuana*. This is a very difficult drug to discuss because of the varieties of marihuana known to exist. The plant grows in almost every section of the world and is easily identified by the number of and characteristically shaped leaves. The plant can grow as high as 8 feet tall. The quality of the intoxicant varies with the location of the plant's growth. There are very weak types of marihuana grown in parts of the country, to stronger types grown in Mexico. Some strains, like those grown in India, are considered potentially dangerous.

Marihuana's chemical name is *Cannabis sativa.* It is called Mary Jane, hay, tea, pot, grass, weed, and a multitude of other names. It is usually smoked, but recently (because adults have become rather sophisticated in detecting the odor) it has been placed in foods, cookies, and candies. The latter method is not popular with the "weed head" who is seeking the quickest intoxication route. Some people who smoke marihuana get sick; others are not so readily affected by the substance; and still others become high.

Parents are faced with the comparison being made between marihuana and alcohol by young adults. Qualitatively and quantitatively, alcohol and marihuana are different. One or two martinis could scarcely intoxicate 10 adults if the two drinks were shared. On the other hand, one "good grade" marihuana cigarette could intoxicate the entire group. When one continues to drink, there is the relief of drunkenness and unconsciousness. There is no such relief with marihuana.

Probably the much abused and maligned discussion concerning the legalization of marihuana will continue.

There is certainly general acceptance of the concept that one with small amounts of marihuana should not be jailed as a criminal.

However, one wonders the wisdom of legalizing a substance that is not fully understood, whose long-term effects are not fully known, and whose dependent characteristics for those who have such tendencies have exhibited themselves consistently or whose general availability and use could open the floodgates of more problems! Certainly America has enough with its alcohol problems without opening the gates to further drug abuse and dependency.

A marihuana user can be detected by the odor of the substance, which, like nicotine, will permeate the clothing and the air. Also, there will be a dilation of the pupils, which often prompts the use of dark or sunglasses. Frequent users develop an inordinate desire for sweets, and studies seem to indicate there is a loss of motivational drive that is detected in lower grades, lack of initiative, and the development of an "I-don't-give-a-damn" attitude.

SUMMARY

The world is filled with exciting and beautiful things. Our country is further filled with tremendous potentials for earnings, accomplishments, and advancement. Regardless of the pressures, the apparent intolerance of pain and discomfort, drugs at the very best alleviate only temporarily.

Under the care of a physician drugs can heal; abused or used indiscriminately, they harm and can even kill. Perhaps the concept that should permeate the field is that "The medicine cabinet that is filled with health is also filled with death."

Chapter 4

INDUSTRIAL ALTERNATIVES

The rationale for establishing an industrial program on alcoholism and drug abuse is not based on the wide spread problems faced nationally, but on the devastating effects on the local company or organization. Regardless of the size or location, the influence of alcohol and drug abuse, alcoholism and addiction, cannot be avoided. Management, employees, and their families are all susceptible, directly or indirectly, to the effects of these insidious problems, and consequently it is a significant concern within the industrial or business complex.

The older generation of managers, executives, and supervisors is rather comfortable with drinking and while not officially accepting the problem as an illness or business concern is somehow understanding that its presence is a possibility. Drugs are something else. Many of those in authority know little about drugs. They may not be ready to accept the fact that young workers who have lived through the drug culture of the 1960s are entering the work force with knowledge of, exposure to, and perhaps usage of drugs.

The existence and prevalence of the drug culture is not relegated to the streets and the family. It inevitably invades the business community.

Alcohol and drugs can be used irresponsibly and/or pathologically, and this is also true of workers in industry. The differences are mainly in degree rather than kind, and they must be dealt with if safe working conditions and a profitable business are to be maintained.

Irresponsible Use

Irresponsible use of alcohol and chemicals may be exhibited by *frequent tardiness* or *absences* from work. The abuser may also appear on the job, but in *less than full capacity,* trying to recover from a hangover or a bad trip. *Personality clashes* between the affected employee and fellow workers or supervisors might well be a consequence of abuse. *Serious slowdown of production or input* due to the inability of the employee to function at maximum efficiency might occur. The greatest danger, however, lies in *safety hazards* created by the employee who works in highly dangerous and hazardous areas of production, and who is made incompetent by alcohol or drugs. Not only can a miscalculation prove to be injurious or fatal to the afflicted employee, but a menace to company property, and more importantly, to the other employees. Regardless of the cause of the injury, the company is liable, which can add insult and compound injury (financial and otherwise).

Pathological Use

Some of the pathological consequences could involve *legal ramification.* The discovery of illegal drugs and or paraphernalia on company premises is embarrassing, potentially dangerous, and a concern of law enforcement. The shadow of suspicion may well begin to hover over the enterprise, thrusting management on the proverbial "horns of a dilemma."

Other difficulties that may arise from alcoholism and drug abuse are *unnecessarily high labor turnovers, substandard production, poor employee morale and internal strife, poor public relations, excessive labor trouble, accidents, errors, loss of equipment,* and *increased cost of liability coverage.*

Industry's Choices

A company or business has three alternatives in dealing with the problems of alcoholism and drug abuse.

One approach is to *deny that the problems exist* within the confines of the company or organization or that *it is even possible for them to exist.* Denying that alcoholism or drug abuse does or might exist is both ridiculous and absurd. It is an immature stand that strips the company and staff from membership in life itself, from the wholesomeness and problems that affect members of the human race, and from illnesses and enigmas of every category. Such a denial is admission of ignorance or perpetuation of the rationalization process that falsely builds one's ego or alibis away one's own fears and problems.

A second method of "handling" the problems of alcoholism and drug abuse is that of *terminating any detected offender.* This principle works on the assumption that the alcoholic or drug abuser is weakwilled, useless, and untreatable, that he or she is an individual who can bring nothing but disgrace and financial loss to the company or organization. Nothing is farther from the truth. Such attitude and subsequent action deprive the company or organization from the benefits of its investment in the individual employee. It is not only economically wasteful but humanly disasterous. No one can deny that there are individuals who are "hopeless" or who refuse assistance when it is offered, and will not change their behavior or alter their performance record. They not only should but *must be terminated.* A business is no haven for drunks and addicts, nor a rehabilitation center for castaway workers. But some mechanism for offering assistance to the troubled worker is certainly the better method of approach, for it invloves a valuable and skilled worker and human being.

The third alternative is *admitting that the possibility exists, realizing that the company or organization has no more immunity than any other industry, and establishing a company program.* Realizing that a problem may be possible is not enough. One could employ a "geographic cure," which would eliminate the source in one specific plant, location, or department, only to put off the inevitable and cause headaches in another area.

The only sensible approach is to have a written company policy and program, offering assistance capable of returning the employee to his or her full potential. This is not only humane but economically sound as well.

It is equally important at the onset to realize that there are some individuals who will refuse assistance and treatment, who do not want to change, and who will continue to be poor performers. For these, when danger exists to company production, time is lost, costly errors are prevalent, or safety is jeopardized, there is only one solution—termination. It is the final approach to the problem, to be taken only after all efforts have failed.

Investment

Every employee—executive, skilled, or unskilled—represents a substantial investment to management and industry. A representative of a national organization estimated 10 years ago that the lowest person on the business "totem pole" was an investment of at least $8000 to the firm. How much more would a chemist, physicist, or an executive with long years of experience be worth? And how much more on today's inflated market?

Usually a person who becomes involved in alcoholism or drug abuse is of the upper or middle echelon of society and industry, who is exposed to entertainment, public relations, contacts, peer pressures, or tension-filled situations that require extraordinary skill, knowledge, and experience. Hence in identifying the problem drinker we are speaking of key individuals even if they are in the ranks.

One might well ask the following questions as it pertains to your company:

1. How much would it cost to replace your company's president? Industrial relations executive? Your immediate boss?
2. Consider the five most productive executives on your payroll. What would it cost to replace one, two, or all five?
3. Choose the 10 most valuable workers. If one or all had to be replaced, what would it cost?

Whatever the enormous price, there exists the possibility that replacement is not available. So it is economically sound to salvage the salvagable, redirect the redirectable, and rehabilitate the rehabilitatable, rather than eliminate the potentially valuable, skilled, and productive employee.

COMPANY PROGRAM

A company program is not impossible. It is very simple, consisting of:

1. *A company policy,* spelling out the company's or organization's rules, regulations, and policies concerning alcoholism, drug abuse, and the troubled employee. It can spell out the steps to be taken, disciplinary actions, available health resources and support, and other criteria surrounding the company's concern for its employees and their problems.
2. *Supervisory training,* with planned programs for everyone at the supervisory level down to the line foreman. The program might well include top management and all employees. Training in the techniques of problem detection and poor performance identification plus the art of handling such problem cases are most important. This is the core portion of the program.
3. *Referral system,* within or outside the company, should be established, made known to key personnel, and utilized so that problem employees can be adequately and efficiently assisted. Naturally, such a program requires the participation and cooperation of labor and management, the medical, personnel, and executive departments; the total work force; and community resources.

COMPANY POLICY

To give force to an industrial alcohol or drug program, the first step should be to have a written policy concerning alcoholism and drug abuse, recognizing them as health problems to be dealt with in the same manner as any other illness. Time off would be allowed for treatment, as for a virulent infection or pneumonia. This implies that the alcoholic or abuser is not only sick, but also treatable. It also implies a deep interest in the employee and his or her family, who may be suffering from a disease that may not have been caused by their doing. It is the only logical solution to the problem.

Acceptance by top management that alcoholism and drug abuse can and do exist, that they are illnesses, that alcoholics and abusers can cause severe damage to production, morale, and safety, that alcoholics and abusers can be salvaged and remain useful and productive members of the industrial team, and that the afflicted employees will not be terminated per se because they come forward for help or are detected will create a closer-knit business family where trust, confidence, and morale will prevail. Workers appreciate the personal interest given to their problems, whatever they may be, and will place more confidence in their supervisors. They will soon come forward more readily for assistance, create a climate of greater cooperation, and consequently assist in the elimination of problems that will lead not only to happier workers but to a more productive work force.

The adopting of the disease concept of alcoholism and drug abuse is the first step in the initiation and support of an alcohol and drug abuse program. It need not be an elaborate outline. An understanding and sympathetic approach to human needs is all that is required in setting up the first and basic requisite of the program.

Perhaps the most important aspect of an overall industrial program is to have top management aware of the possibility of the prevalence of alcoholism and drug abuse, what they can do to the industry's finances, and, of equal importance, what they can do to their individual employees. Since alcoholism and abuse thrive in the upper echelon of society, it is likely that the same will exist more frequently within the managerial level than in any other department of the business. Alcoholism and drug abuse play a significant part of any sound and comprehensive safety program. The effect of alcohol and drug abuse on behavior and skills is sufficient reason to have top management insure their inclusion in the company's educational program.

THE COMPANY TRAINING PROGRAM

In order for the program to be effective, all personnel involved in its operation must be aware of the functions and procedures. This necessitates an adequate and comprehensive training program, especially for the supervisors who will be encountering the poor work performance caused by alcohol and drugs. Another reason for the need of training is the possible resistance to the program by supervisors. They may be reluctant to cooperate because they feel alcohol and drugs are moral issues, and those who indulge in their use are "sinners," outside the prerogative of the supervisor.

An honest attempt must be made to educate them to the fact that alcohol and drug abusers are physically sick and need help, and that the supervisors can play a tremendous part in their recovery and restoration to full capacity. In carrying out duties of supervisors, the approach will be strictly on performance. The supervisor is no diagnostician or therapist. However, he or she can and must sustain and improve performance and output. It is on this basis that the troubled employee is brought to task and hopefully to a recovery program.

The supervisor may feel uncomfortable in carrying out company policy because of his or her close relationship with these employees, many of whom he or she may drink with socially. Again, through the company program, the supervisor will be taught how to differentiate between "use" and "abuse."

There is another difficulty in enlisting the supervisor's participation in the program. The fear of "squealing" on a fellow worker, in identifying a problem of performance, oftentimes dilutes the supervisor's desire to maintain good production. The company program is no witch hunt, no squealing. It in fact protects the employee from further deterioration and ultimate termination.

If the supervisor does not understand what the company policy toward alcohol and drug abuse is, he or she will have difficulty enforcing it. Everyone's business soon becomes no one's business. The problems of confrontation, authority, approach, and referral must be handled as routinely as securing material or signing for overtime. The supervisor will need to know how far (hopefully all the way) upper management will go when the company policy is initiated. What to do, when to do it, why do it, and how to do it, must be reviewed by all personnel in supervisory capacity until their actions become second nature. Then the program becomes workable and results can be expected.

LEGAL ASPECTS

If the concern about production, profit, employee well-being, safety, plant or office morale, and community enhancement are not sufficient motivation to prompt company action in the field of alcohol abuse, drug abuse, and related people problems, then legal considerations should.

What would be your company's legal liability should limb or life be lost by an accident precipitated by a worker under the influence of alcohol or drugs?

How liable and to what degree would your business be if someone is injured or killed by a company driver on company business on company time who is legally intoxicated or appreciably under the influence of alcohol?

How would the courts view an accident by a company-employed driver who is on methadone?

To what extent would a business be responsible for the injury or death of an employee hurt or killed returning home from a company party where alcohol was being served?

What is the legal responsibility in seeing that excesses do not occur at a company function?

Would the appropriate governmental agencies and courts uphold your company's termination of an alcoholic or drug abuser?

To what extent is a company responsible to prevent illegal and ill-used legal drugs on location?

Is it acceptable to fire someone who is in possession of an illegal drug or a policy-prohibited bottle of alcohol?

Is preemployment drug screening legal?

Some Answers

In a decision rendered (94 Cal. App. 2nd p. 477) the court ruled that an employer who operated a dry cleaning business had tolerated drinking by his workers during regular afternoon breaks. Empty bottles were used to store cleaning fluid. At an informal holiday party, an employee mistakenly drank from a bottle containing cleaning fluid and died. The court upheld that the injury was work related, and the company was held liable.

In another case involving an Arnold Tate, janitor, who accompanied his supervisor on a work-related mission, stopped for a few drinks, completed his office work, and subsequently continued drinking with the supervisor, and lost his life in a traffic accident while intoxicated, the court ruled the employer was liable.

In the now-famous California Supreme Court case, the court upheld that the injury and death of one Daniel McCarty who was killed when he drove home from a Christmas party given by his employer occurred in the scope of employment.

This is a most interesting case, in view of the following circumstances that surrounded the case: most employees left early from the party that was located at a special meeting place. McCarty himself returned home, picked up additional liquor, returned to the office party, passed his bottle around, continued to drink from company stock, became ill, and when he awoke visibly intoxicated, both a foreman and fellow worker offered to drive him home, which he refused. Blood alcohol level at the time of death was 0.26%.

As per the ruling of the court, the party was on company premises, endorsed expressly or implied, since it was an official company activity, and it was not necessary to show expressed consent for such occasions as parties, for allowing drinks on the premise served as implied consent of approval on the part of the employer.

In most cases, general preemployment drug screening is legal, as long as it is required for the performance of all job applicants on a nondiscriminatory basis.

One can readily see the need of company policy and procedures as regards alcohol and drug problems from a legal standpoint. It is not only the "in" thing to do, but it is actually the "must" thing.

REFERRAL

Finally, in developing a referral system care must be taken so that all needs of the troubled employee and his or her family can be met. Such resources might include assistance for:

Emergency cases
Crisis situations
Nonemergency cases
Detoxification cases
Counseling and rehabilitation cases
Family involvement

Every private, public, and governmental agency should be incorporated in the system to make the resources all-inclusive.

SUMMARY

As stated previously, a company program is not difficult to implement. Its foundation rests on the humanitarian and financial concerns any business should have. It is a practical approach to an unavoidable problem—troubled employees. It places alcohol and drug problems with the host of other problems that have been recognized as trouble areas and that have been handled as a performance problem.

Chapter 5

POLICY

Policy is the foundation upon which a company operates. It spells out the *when, where,* and *how.* Without it, business flounders and stability is impossible. While some companies, usually smaller ones, rely on verbal policies, probably made when decisions become necessary, it is far better to have written policies to deal with important aspects of the business machinery. The same pertains to policies regarding alcoholism and drug abuse.

It is the duty of top management, including the board of directors, president, or owner, if they are applicable to the situation, to be part of the policy development. Valuable assistance can be obtained from such national agencies as the National Council on Alcoholism and the Occupational Branch of the National Institute on Alcohol Abuse and Alcoholism, as well as from companies that have long years of experience with such matters. Most have weathered the storm of challenges and can supply practical suggestions which can stand the test of trial and time.

The role of labor is important in the development of policy. One method is the establishment of a task force which will put together the ingredients of a policy which will be sound and workable. When labor and management have contributed in the establishment of company policy the chances of it succeeding are enhanced.

Once the policy has been accepted by the company and its appropriate executives and members, then it is the duty of management to interpret the policy to every level of employment, down to the individual employees. Everyone within the complex must know that the policy is supported by top management and by the union if one exists, that the offer of services and assistance are meant, that the confidentiality of service will be maintained, that no one will suffer adversely should they seek for themselves or members of their families assistance for a related alcohol and/or drug problem. The company's intent to help must be clearly understood so no one will be frightened by any phase of the program.

The goal of the alcoholism program or drug program, or both, should be clear. It is not abstinence, nor a witch hunt that is being promoted. Responsible use of alcohol and drugs are the objectives (Chart 5.1).

If indeed anything is being combatted, it is irresponsible and pathological use of alcohol and drugs, both of which are detrimental to the individual and the company.

What should be included in a company policy?

ALCOHOLISM POLICY

It is important that each company develop its own policy to deal with alcohol abuse, alcoholism, and the presence

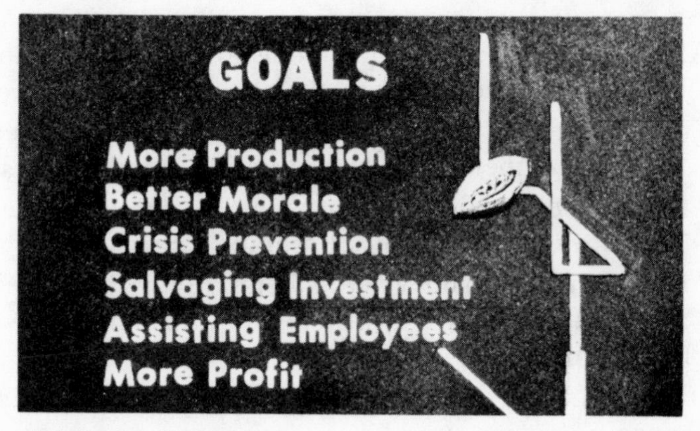

Chart 5.1 Goals of a Program

of drugs on the premises. The following might be included as statements in such a policy:

Alcoholism or problem drinking is an illness to be considered as such and treated as such.

Alcoholism can strike anyone, at any age, at any status of employment.

Alcoholism is not a sign of weakness but an illness that is treatable.

Most problem drinkers in industry are valuable employees who can and should be helped.

Early detection is important for company and individual benefit to assure early diagnosis and treatment, and thus enhance recovery.

Problem drinkers are extended the identical health and medical benefits as those suffering from any other problem or illness.

Management is dedicated to helping problem drinkers, and encourages acceptance of treatment.

Regular sickness benefits may be paid when the employee is hospitalized or at home or at a rehabilitation center approved as such, being treated for problem drinking.

Alcoholism and related problems are covered by the company's medical plan.

Employees are encouraged to seek help for their family members, for alcoholism is a family illness.

There is no social or employment stigma associated with problem drinking or seeking help for it.

Alcoholism in terms of the company is an illness that adversely affects the work performance of the employee.

Diagnosis and treatment outside the company are encouraged.

It is the responsibility of supervisors to be alert to all instances of alcohol abuse and alcoholism that might be indicated by lack of work performance.

The program within the company is to be based solely on performance. No supervisor is a recognized diagnostician.

The utilization of the company's resources for the handling of such problems is encouraged.

Refusal to follow direction and correct performance problems will lead to the same disciplinary action taken for any other work-related problem.

Strict confidentiality of records and information will be maintained and acceptance of treatment shall in no way interfere with justified promotions and advancements.

Bringing of alcoholic beverages on location is prohibited by company policy and is sufficient cause for dismissal because of the inherent hazards.

Drug Policy

Drug policies differ again from company to company, and may contain some of the following items:

The possession, sale, or use of illegal drugs on company premises is sufficient cause for dismissal.

The company will not hire anyone who is a known drug user. It will consider those who have successfully coped with their problem for employment.

Security personnel will be incorporated in the company's detection efforts.

Any violation of the drug laws on company time or premises can be cause for dismissal from employment.

Any former employee terminated for a drug-abuse-related problem may be reinstated only with the approval of the medical director and the personnel director.

Drug abuse will be considered as a health problem and is to be handled and treated by the company as such.

Drug abuse can strike anyone, at any age, and at any status of employment.

Compulsory drug education programs will be initiated for employees at all levels.

The medical and nursing departments will play an important part in the company's detection program.

Medical examinations will be made a compulsory part of the company employee health package, to afford appropriate medical supervision and detection.

Preemployment screening process will be established, which may include urinalysis for all applicants.

Urinalysis will be made a part of the regular physical checkup policies and procedures of the company.

Anyone found with illegal drugs on company property will be terminated.

Payment for treatment of employees with drug habits and abuse, and rehabilitation of them shall be borne by the company as in the case of any other health problem.

All help afforded by the company shall be on a strictly confidential basis.

Seeking help for a drug abuse problem shall not jeopardize any possible employment promotion or advancement.

Employees are urged to seek help for drug problems that may affect themselves or members of their families.

The program within the company is to be based on performance and possession of drugs. The supervisor is not a recognized diagnostician.

The utilization of company and communtiy resources is encouraged.

Refusal to follow direction and correct performance problems due to drug abuse or any other problem will lead to the same disciplinary action taken for any other work-related problem.

TYPES OF COMPANY PROGRAMS

Large companies have often seen fit to appoint an *employee assistance coordinator* whose responsibility it is to see that the occupational program geared to help the troubled employee is initiated, activated, and implemented. Some large companies have even hired their own treatment team of social workers, psychologists, and physicians to afford in-house rehabilitation and treatment. This is indeed a luxury, and not always the most effective manner to approach the problem. Certainly it is not the least expensive.

Other companies have utilized the services of local alcoholism councils or committees, mental health centers, and other groups, including private consultants to help formulate their policies, and to train their supervisory staff, who ultimately will be making identification of performance problems. Some of these consultants and agencies are available for discussion with troubled employees, to help guide the individual or member of the family to an appropriate local resource, or in some cases to out-of-town resources.

Regardless of the approach, the important thing is to activate the program through policy development and supervisory training, which ulitmately will lead to early identification and referral to appropriate facilities.

The following is a typical company policy on alcoholism and drug abuse—source unknown:

POLICY ON ALCOHOLISM AND DRUG ABUSE

The ______________________________ and its employee committees adopt the following policy applicable to all employees who may be adversely affected by alcoholism, problem drinking, or other addictive patterns that may contribute to deteriorating job performance or balanced living.

1. The ______________________________ and its employee committees recognize that alcoholism is a progressive illness that is treatable. Any employee having this illness will receive the same careful consideration and offer of treatment that is extended to employees who suffer other illnesses.
2. The referral service provided under this policy

will be available to family members as well as to employees.

3. Alcoholism is defined under this policy as an illness in which an employee's consumption of any alcoholic beverage definitely and repeatedly interferes with job performance or health. This definition applies to the use of any mood-changing chemicals having similar adverse effects.
4. This policy does not apply to social drinking.
5. No employee with a drinking problem will have his or her job security or promotional opportunities jeopardized by a request for diagnosis or treatment. The records relating to treatment under this program will be kept confidential.
6. Supervisors are not expected to diagnose medical behavioral problems.
7. It is expected through this policy that employees who suspect they may have a medical behavioral problem, even in its early stages, will be encouraged to seek diagnosis and, when indicated, follow through with the prescribed treatment. Successful treatment requires a high degree of motivation. This policy is designed to promote a climate of trust and confidence wherein such motivation can be achieved. The objective of the program is to assist employees who may develop alcoholism or drug problems to help themselves in arresting its further advance before the condition results in lack of capability.
8. This program does not supplant the normal discipline and grievance procedures.
9. This policy and its implementation will be administered by a joint labor-management committee.

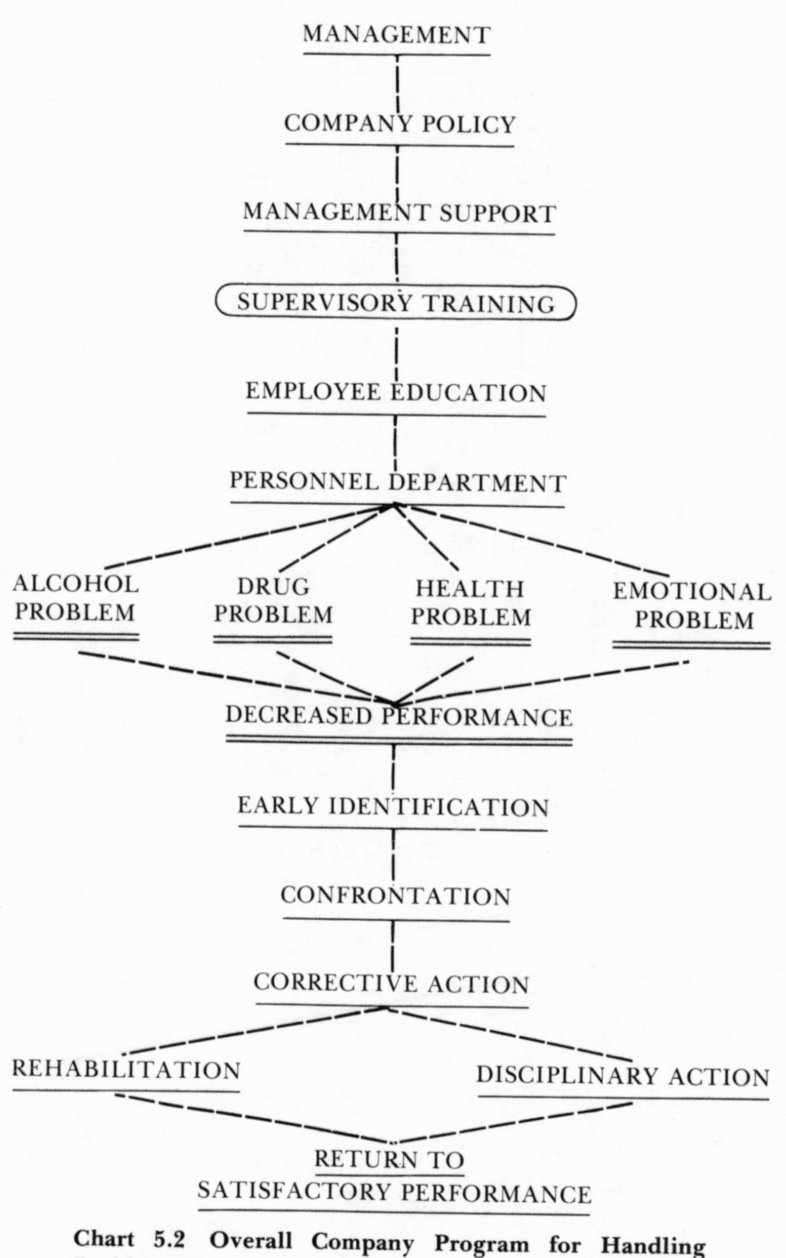

Chart 5.2 Overall Company Program for Handling Problem Employees

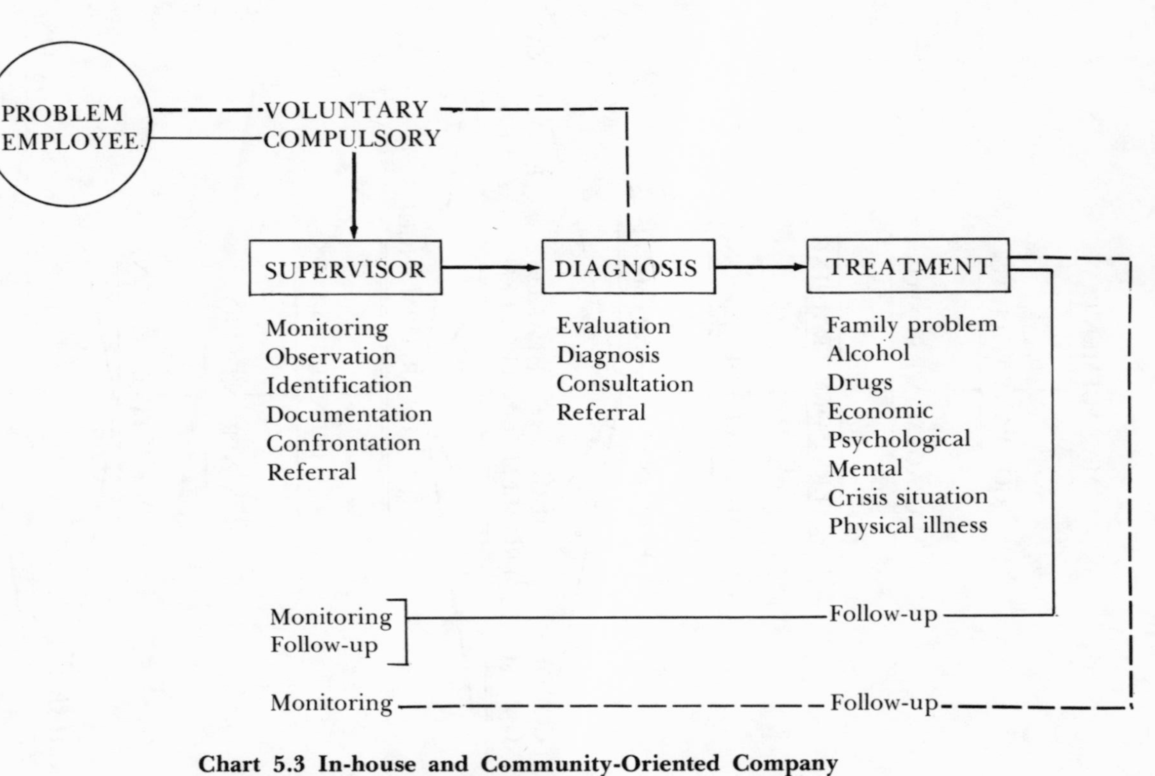

Chart 5.3 In-house and Community-Oriented Company Plan for Handling Troubled Employees

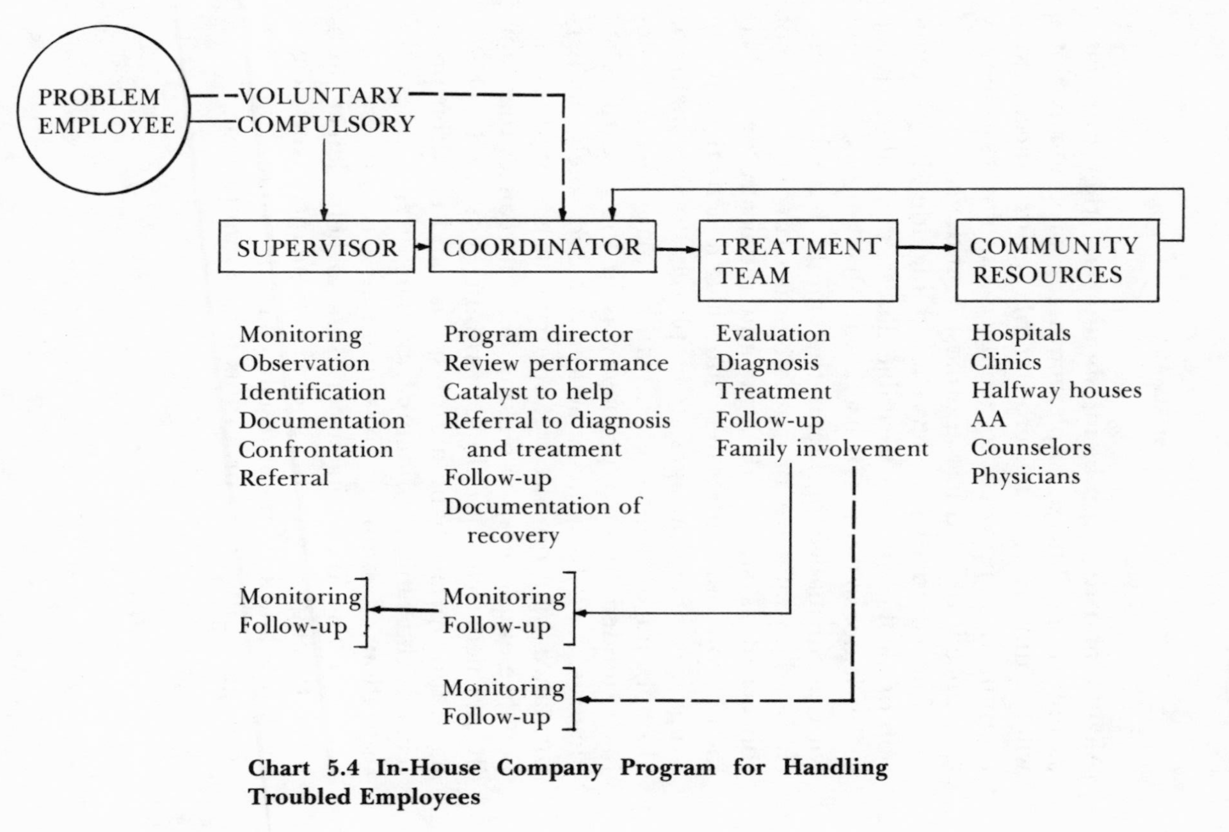

Chart 5.4 In-House Company Program for Handling Troubled Employees

Summary

Alcohol and drug problems should have the same status as any other illness. Implementing a program is not a witch hunt. It is a monitoring of performance, and a nonpunitive approach to troubled employees whereby assistance is offered in the utmost confidence.

The company's policy should include the recognition of alcoholism as a treatable illness; drug abuse is the same; it doesn't concern itself with drinking as such but with performance problems that might have been precipitated by abusive or pathological drinking; it is not concerned as such with legal and medically prescribed medication but with safety and illegal activities in the drug area; it encourages its employees to seek help for alcohol and drug problems, with company health benefits extended to such problems as in the case of other illnesses; any disciplinary action is based solely on performance, not on alcohol or drug usage; it does not penalize employees for seeking help; it realizes that family problems can also hinder productivity, and encourages appropriate handling of spouse and children problems in the same confidential manner; it encourages the utilization of company and community resources; it encourages and trains its supervisors to help detect problems through signs of poor performance, and leaves diagnosis and treatment to clinicians; it prompts and encourages educational programs for all employees.

Chapter 6

THE SUPERVISORY FORCE

THE KEY—THE SUPERVISORY STAFF

The key to a successful industrial program is the supervisory staff. This segment of the business complex is the focal point of any plant or company endeavor, for it is the core fusing management with labor, policy with production, and the business establishment with the workers.

If management—the loose, cumbersome term used to denote the controlling and governing group—commands, the supervisory staff carrries out the orders. Communication and liaison, understanding, and loyalty must permeate the atmosphere in any company undertaking.

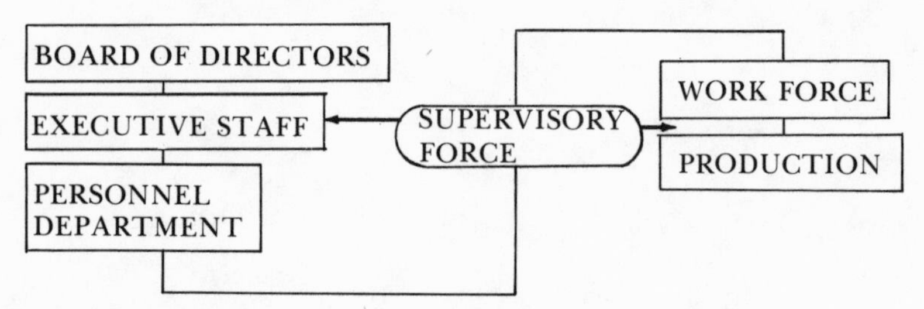

Chart 6.1 Company organizational structure

The basic organizational structure of any large business consits of a board of directors, the executive staff, the personnel department (including the medical department), the supervisory force, and the work force (see Chart 6.1). The role of the supervisor in the overall structure of the company or business is clearly crucial. Supervisors not only hold a unique position in a company, but also the most important. Upon them rests the dual responsibility of looking out for the welfare of the company and of the work force. Their responsibility is so important that on its efficiency rests the effectiveness of the work force and the ultimate production and profit.

Supervisors owe loyalty to the company, which includes the fulfillment of the responsibility to achieve maximum production from the work force and detect and remedy anything that is detrimental to the vested interest of the employer.

On the other hand, responsibility to the people directly under command demands awareness and interest for their welfare, safety, health, and happiness to the extent of business and at times even personal relationships.

On both counts, the detection and the remedying of alcohol and drug problems become a most important task of the supervisor. Hiding the problem drinker, the alcoholic, or the drug user only embezzles valuable time, production, and profits from an employer who has put trust in the supervisor's leadership; hiding not only opens the door for costly accidents and possible death, and exposes other workers to injury, but also does a severe injustice to the employee who is suffering from a progressive disease that will not remain stagnant but progresses until ultimate destruction is attained. In addition to the monetary loss and potential physical dangers, the troubled employee will, because of excuses, rationalizations, and hiding by a supervisor, ultimately lose health, family, financial stability, and even life.

Dual Responsibility

The dual responsibility of the supervisor, who could be from the point of command to the level of line supervisor, demands, therefore, loyalty to the company and to the work force. It is this very loyalty that poses the greatest threat to the effective accomplishment of the supervisor's role.

Americans have an innate hatred of "squealing." Hence, for the most part, supervisors are prone to hide, excuse, rationalize, and belittle problems of their subordinates, particularly close friends. Alcoholism is one such potentially excuse-laden problem. "Mike was only sick." "Joe needs a check to cover family needs." "Sam is a fine fellow. Known him all my life." "How can I expose Jim? I know his wife and kids so well." "Tom, go sleep it off. I'll pinch hit for you." And so it goes.

Supporting the employee is an excellent trait. Loyalty is usually returned by loyalty and better production. Saving a person's job is a noble act. However, when the alcoholic or drug addict is hidden, excused, or allowed to continue his or her self-disguised "antics," it is not a simple case of whitewashing a friend's mistake. It is actually allowing an illness to gnaw away at the victim's health and happiness. For alcoholism and drug abuse destroy not only physical health, but also mental, social, spiritual, and economic well being as well.

Alcoholism or drug addiction is progressive, with steady increases in the danger signals and involvement. To conceal them is to condemn the victim to the insidious ravages of an illness that will destroy all facets of life. The realization that detection is the greatest favor a supervisor can offer a subordinate, with the understanding that anything short of this is unfair not only to the company but to the "friend" in question, is the foundation of the program.

Alcoholics and drug abusers can cause serious accidents not only to themselves but to others as well. Tragedies don't just happen. They are too heavy a price to pay for failure of duty in detecting serious problems.

Again, as we move up the ladder of industry, the possibility of alcoholism and drug abuse becomes more probable. Supervisors earn more than subordinates; executives still more. It is important that the leaders realize the facts about alcohol and drugs and the danger signs of alcoholism and addiction.

Detecting The Alcoholic And Drug-Abusing Employee

Supervisors are in an excellent position to detect problems, as are members of the personnel and medical staffs.

On-the-job clues that are exhibited early in the illness and indicate problems are:

1. *Absenteeism.* Particularly Mondays and the day after payday. This can be on a half-day basis, with the employee venturing to work and

being unable to continue past the noon hour. Blame is placed on a virus infection, migrane headaches, cramps, and the like. Of course Monday is usually a difficult day for the alcoholic or drug user. Even early in his or her illness there is a hung-over or tripped-out feeling, and the employee can only give half his or her potentials—if not less.

2. *Temporary departures from the job.* This is a very convenient manner for the alcoholic or addict to get a "shot." If not one of these problems is the reason, it can indicate some other difficulty.
3. *Unsual excuses.* Usually to cover up an employee's absence. Alcoholics and abusers can come up with the most unique and outlandish excuses: the car won't start, the engine overheated, the car had a flat, a blowout, ran out of gas, the fan belt broke, the wheel fell off, the engine burned out, and so on; a pattern of anything and everything covers up the real problem.
4. *Mood changes.* Especially after long meal breaks. Continual moods of glowing exhilaration, or change of normal personality traits is usually a sign of something out of the ordinary.
5. *Red or bleary eyes.* This can be a normal characteristic, but probably is not likely. This "hangover" characteristic can be the point of detecting the problem. Perhaps the person has eye problems.
6. *Lower quality of work.* Any sickness or emotional strain can be the source of this employment problem. When it becomes evident that there is an association with drinking or drugs, it is indicative of a problem; at any rate, regard-

less of the cause, it is too serious a sign to let "ride." Alcoholics and drug abusers find it difficult to keep up high quality of work because of the physical strain alcoholism and drug abuse cause. Again, this is true of the employee who will find it impossible to give his or her fullest to the job at hand because of the strain encountered at home with an alcoholic or addicted spouse or child.

7. *Loud talking.* When this occurs, especially after lunch, it is a possible indication of release of inhibitions, or at least of some unusual exhibition. It should be noted, particularly if it occurs under similar circumstances on a regular basis.
8. *Lunch drinking.* When an employee begins to drink more and more at lunch or is absent from the usual place of eating to visit an establishment where drinks are served, something might be brewing. The employee is changing his or her pattern.
9. *Long breaks.* When indulged either in the plant or at lunch, it is a sign of a problem. Perhaps it is laziness, some stress, hiding drinks or a "stash," or sleeping a few moments—which are unfair to the company and to other workers.
10. *Rapid drinking.* Gulping drinks, as has been already mentioned, is a possible indication of an abnormal condition.
11. *Suspiciousness.* It can indicate a problem if an employee is suspicious of or if unable to place confidence in his or her superior, depending on the degree of suspicion. If the suspicion approaches paranoia, either the supervisor is at fault or the worker is suffering from some mental block or problem, if not alcoholism or

addiction, or some other accompanying mental health condition. In either case, it is important that the problem be detected and resolved.

12. *Tremors.* These are seemingly "cured" by coffee breaks. Caffeine can scarcely calm an individual who is nervous.
13. *Excessive nervousness.* While not necessarily a conclusive sign of alcohol or drug abuse, this can indicate a problem, either mental or physical. Either is grounds enough to alert and hopefully render assistance.
14. *Increased tolerance for alcohol.* This is quite noticeable. Although perhaps not indicative of a problem, unless intoxication follows habitually, it is a sign that alcohol is playing a more significant role in the person's life and is worthy of careful attention.
15. *Denial.* When the drinking gets out of hand or increases and the supervisor knows it is a cause of difficulty but the employee denies it. The same would be true for drug usage.

Later signs of problems that are exhibited on the job are:

16. *Spasmodic work pace.* The alcoholic and drug user is notorious for this. On "hung-over"or "tripped-out" days, the employee is slow and very deliberate. He or she endeavors to make up for his or her slowness by double speed. This is abnormal behavior and certainly should be studied carefully.
17. *Lower quantity of work.* The alcohol or drug abuser is unable to produce as quickly as before. This is also the case of the employee with an alcoholic or addicted spouse or child.

18. *Hangovers on the job.* If habitual, it is indicative of a problem. Furthermore, here enters the safety factor regarding performance.
19. *Breath purifiers.* The alcoholic uses these to hide the odor of alcohol. Some individuals like gum, mints, and the like.
20. *Financial problems.* When money becomes a problem for the alcoholic or drug user, debts are incurred and large loans are sometimes made from the company or from the retirement plan. This behavior may result from some other health problem or emergency, but it certainly cannot be denied if it occurs over a long period of time. It could result from excessive drinking or drug abuse since it is the typical pattern of alcoholics and drug users.
21. *Depressed condition.* It is not normal for an individual to be depressed habitually. There is a cause: problems, poor health, or perhaps alcoholism or drug abuse.
22. *Drinking or popping pills on the job.* This is a real indication of a drinking or a drug problem. Alcoholics and addicts hide their drinks in thermos bottles, desk drawers, and the like. Safety and efficiency are involved here.
23. *Avoidance of supervisors and workers.* Humans are social beings, for the most part; hence such behavior is indication of trouble. The trouble may not necessarily be alcoholism or drug abuse. It is a sign of impending difficulty, for there is usually a reason for this behavior.
24. *Flushed face.* Unless it is a normal trait of the individual, it could be a sign of high blood pressure or excessive drinking.

25. *Increased occurrence of real minor illnesses.* When absenteeism becomes a serious problem or constant visits to the infirmary is routine, the situation is worth investigating.
26. *Family problems.* Regardless of the cause, it is an industrial omen—less efficiency, less production, unhappiness, potential accidents, and so on.
27. *Resentfulness.* There is always a reason for this unnatural exhibition. It may necessitate a personal inventory on the supervisor's part or it may be a matter for the employee to study.
28. *Losing tools and materials.* If done to excess, this can be a signal of a problem.
29. *Neglecting details,* which once were so perfectly done.
30. *Intoxicated on the job.* How can one miss this?
31. *Increasing number of errors.*
32. *Slowdown in production.* When the rest of the work force is increasing its output, this can indicate a problem if habitual.

Off the job, the supervisor can sometimes note signs of problems brewing: excessive drinking, spending too much money or time drinking, marital discord, police involvement, habitual late hours away from home, resentfulness exhibited toward neighbors, habitual drunkenness, disruption of family and church activities, covering up drinking, drunkenness, or drug usage by self and family, particularly the older children and spouse.

Difficult Problem

Detecting signs of danger may be a comparatively easy task. Pinpointing the diagnosis is not so easy. Only a trained professional and the victim can really outline the problem.

The signs of alcoholism, drug abuse, and their progressive traits develop so slowly at times that they can escape detection. Furthermore the supervisor's own ignorance or attitudes can do much to hamper proper detection and approach.

If the lines of communications are not well established, it will be a difficult task for the supervisor to approach the worker. The worker will tend to excuse, hide, and do everything short of losing his or her own job to prevent termination.

Many supervisors feel most inadequate in their ability to evaluate, and this is the alibi used for turning their heads from the problem drinker and the drug abuser.

Should the offer of help be refused, and production or work performance continues to suffer, the supervisor owes it to all concerned to follow through with further action, disciplinary moves, and termination.

Termination will, in certain cases, save lives that could have been lost in an accident, prevent loss to the company by poor work, and even save the employee's life, family, and future. It could motivate the employee to seek help. If all appeals fail, at least the supervisor will have the comfort of knowing he or she did all that was possible to help.

Knowing detection techniques of abuse is irrelevant. What is pertinent is detection of poor performance, safety hazards, and general personnel and production problems.

Supervisor Meetings

The method to attain an effective alcoholism program is through supervisory staff meetings that would emphasize the following:

1. The supervisor's important role in the company.
2. The supervisor's dual responsibility.
3. Attitudes toward drinking and drugs.
4. Physiology of alcohol and drugs—safety aspects.
5. Alcoholism, drug addiction, and abuse—definitions, danger signs, and statistics.
6. How to detect the alcoholic and drug abuser, from a performance basis.
7. How to approach the alcoholic and drug abuser who is a poor performer.
8. Referral resources.

Supervisors have a grave responsibility in endeavoring to reach the alcoholic employee. However, the approach should not be on the basis of alcoholism or drug abuse. The stand a supervisor should take in regard to the addiction problem is on the basis of work performance, explaining that from a safety viewpoint or from the production angle there is a need for better work and the elimination of production problems. The supervisor should point out that unless things do change, it will be impossible for the troubled employee to continue working.

A humanitarian appeal can also be used with indications of personal interest and concern for the employee's total welfare. Every opportunity should be given to allow the person to accept help and improve performance. Because the employee is suffering from some problem, the most important part of the entire program is to have the individual referred to some appropriate facility or therapist who will be able to follow through with treatment.

The most comforting phase of alcoholism and drug abuse is the fact that they are treatable illnesses. Alcoholics and drug abusers can be returned to normal living and made useful members of society and productive members of the industrial team.

SUMMARY

The supervisory force is the most important component of any business structure. A company succeeds or fails on the strength or weakness of those in supervision. For this reason, the supervisor is the most important link in any occupational approach to alcohol and drug problems and effective performance.

Detection of the alcoholic employee or drug abuser must be based on performance. While there are many signs of poor performance which are indicative of a possible alcohol or drug problem, the determination of the cause is irrelevant to the importance of performance. Diagnosis must be left to clinicians, who are equipped to make such determinations.

A supervisor's responsibility is to maintain production, lessen and hopefully eliminate safety hazards, and detect performance problems which could not only diminish company profit, but which could ultimately lead to disciplinary problems and ultimate termination of an employee.

An excellent tool to train supervisors in their important company role is to hold regular supervisory meetings. Permeating the substance of the content material to be discussed must be performance, techniques of approaches, referral resources, and the business and humanitarian aspects of the company program.

Finally one must realize that there is a limit to everyone's capacity. Regardless of a supervisor's skill in dealing with an alcohol or drug problem, only an appropriate referral of the worker can reap success. Confrontation is necessary, and appropriate consultation with management and labor must be maintained.

Chapter 7

APPROACHING THE TROUBLED EMPLOYEE

IDENTIFICATION

The troubled employee can be anyone. It could very well be and probably is a person with a long record of service with the company, or one in an important position. Most alcoholic employees are between 35 and 50 years of age, and in companies with low turnovers have been employed for 10 or more years. They are found at every level of employment. Today, young adults bring to industry part of their teen culture, which in some instances reflect exposure to drugs and the drug culture.

Probably the individual in question is intelligent, capable, and gifted—a real or potential asset to the firm. Furthermore, depending on the stage of detection, he or she could be married, a homeowner, a religious person, and of considerable financial status. He or she will exhibit one of the on-the-job and/or off-the-job signs of alcoholism or drug abuse. There will be, at least, some indication of trouble. Hovering over the scene is the consideration that the employee is in *trouble, sick,* but *can be salvaged.*

Because the troubled employee—and particularly the alcoholic and drug abuser—in time becomes fearful, anxious, remorseful, isolated, suspicious, hostile, depressed, resentful, and dependent, utmost tact is necessary in approaching him or her. He or she is sick—in body, mind, and soul—and wrong techniques of approach will only alienate and push the employee deeper into the problem.

The foundation of the program is "work performance." Inevitably signs of deterioration will become manifest. Perhaps not in the early stages, which is unfortunate, but as the problem of alcohol or drug abuse develops, the worker will begin to exhibit work problems. It is in this area that the supervisor should be comfortable. He or she is not a diagnostician, to repeat what has already been mentioned, not a counselor, not an evaluator, but a supervisor of productivity, and if there is something amiss in this area there should be no hesitation in so identifying it.

There are numerous ways in addition to strictly work monitoring that will bring the problem of the troubled employee to the surface, and hopefully to diagnosis and treatment, whether it be through the supervisor, the company employee assistance coordinator, or some local agency. When employees have been consistently kept informed about the company policy and intent, and when educational devices and programs have been shared to the extent that everyone within the company or business becomes conscious of self-evaluation and introspection, not only as it pertains to work performance, but to living—family relationships, financial stability, crisis handling, social contacts, spiritual values, and happiness—progress can be attained.

An example of an Employee Work Performance

Scale, based on self-examination, distributed to employees of companies that have in-house and community-based occupation programs is found on this page.

EMPLOYEE WORK PERFORMANCE SCALE

(A questionnaire for personal problem determination)

1. Are you drinking too much?
2. Are you having marital problems?
3. Is your drinking affecting your attendance at work?
4. Are your family problems affecting your job?
5. Does your drinking adversely affect your relationship with other workers?
6. Is worrying over your children's drug involvement affecting your work?
7. Do you feel like the walls are caving in on you?
8. Are you using drugs to get you "over the hump"?
9. Are you using drugs or medications without proper medical direction?
10. Are you abusing drugs?
11. Are you preoccupied with drinking?
12. Are family concerns infiltrating your work day?
13. Are legal problems causing you to neglect your work?
14. Been picked up for driving while intoxicated?
15. Are debts or financial problems affecting your work?
16. Is your work day filled with worry and concern about your spouse, your spouse's attitude, behavior, illness, drinking, drug taking, and the like?
17. Is the condition of your health or worry

about it interfering with your happiness and productivity?

18. Are you reluctant to seek help to alleviate your condition, problems, or illness?
19. Has life lost its meaning for you?
20. Are problems interfering with your relationship with your boss?

REMEMBER: Everyone has problems.

Some deny their problems, and they (problems) continue to grow.

Others try to escape from their problems through geographic and employment changes and "cures," but the problems follow the victims.

There are some who try to numb the pain of their problems by the "magic" of alcohol or drugs, only to have them return following the chemical metabolism with all of their fury and complications, plus a hangover, and an inevitable chemical problem.

The wise person faces his or her problems and tries to solve them, or if impossible to resolve, learn how to live with them in an atmosphere of acceptance, serenity, and productivity.

Another excellent tool for supervisory and employee consideration is the Ladder of Employee Deterioration, Chart 7.1, found on page 111. The concept is based on the ladder of productivity and failure exemplified in the progressive deterioration of a problem drinker. Signs that are of a personal, family, and work nature are often easily identified and can be of great assistance to the problem drinker in motivating the seeking of help, and the supervisor in observing the developing work pattern.

HEALTH
PERFORMANCE
HAPPINESS

Gross drinking behavior
"Blackouts" following drinking
Diminishing quantity of production
Poor quality of work
Comment from supervisor or boss
Increased personal problems
Family difficulties
Loss of friends
Preoccupation with drinking
Poor attendance
Warning from supervisor
Deterioration of relationships with fellow worker
Loss of advancement opportunity
Borrowing money
Trouble with the law
Confrontation with the boss or supervisor
Punitive disciplinary action
Recurring personal, family, and business crises
Serious family problems
Financial collapse
Loss of family
Total performance deterioration
Binges
Final employment confrontation
Termination
Skid row

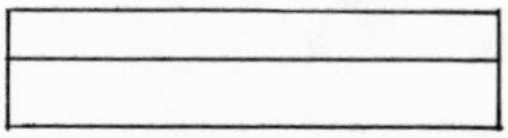

Physical deterioration
Death

Chart 7.1 Ladder of Employee Deterioration (Chart is one of many similar ones used by groups and organizations in outlining employee deterioration.)

MOTIVATION

The crux of the problem lies in motivating the alcohol and/or drug abuser to seek treatment. This can only come from his or her willingness to *surrender* to the fact that there is a problem. There are many therapists who feel that this is the first and only sign indicating a good prognosis. If the problem employee does not desire and accept help, no one can assist that person.

The most characteristic trait of the alcoholic and drug abuser is *denial*—rationalization of the situation, denying that a problem exists, projecting the difficulty to someone else.

"I really didn't miss that many days," he or she might say. "Had to stay up with the wife all night." "The weather has been so cold. Has me feeling under the weather." "Just give me one more chance, and it will work itself out." "My work has been good." "I don't remember the mistakes you speak of, you must be thinking of someone else." And so it goes.

In treatment situations the chant is the same, only directed in a different vein: "It's my wife. If she would only keep quiet! She's always complaining! Always demanding!" "The country is shot! We're going downstream. It's depressing!" "The noise the children make is unbelievable. Can't stand it. That's why I drink." "I'm a moderate drinker. Now my next door neighbor is really a heavy drinker. I think he is an alcoholic." (His neighbor drinks two fifths a day; he only drinks one. He is moderate! His neighbor is immoderate.) "I'm only a little bit alcoholic!" (It's like being only a little bit pregnant. Either you are or you are not.)

Recently, an actively drinking alcoholic told me that he was drinking because of Watergate. He drank before Watergate, during Watergate, and now post-Watergate.

Perhaps no alcoholic voluntarily stops drinking. Vernelle Fox, M.D., former head of the Georgian Clinic in Atlanta, Georgia, and more recently Medical Director of Alcohol Services, Long Beach General Hospital, Long Beach, California, once said,

> "An alcoholic voluntarily stops drinking when his wife says, 'If you don't stop drinking, I'll leave you.' So he voluntarily stops.
> "The sick alcoholic voluntarily stops drinking when his physician tells him, 'If you don't stop drinking, you'll die.' So he voluntarily stops drinking.
> "The problem employee with a drinking problem voluntarily stops drinking when his boss tells him, 'If you don't begin to show better work performance, we'll have to let you go.' He voluntarily stops drinking and seeks help."

The point is that no alcoholic or problem employee redirects his or her life unless there is a reason for doing so. Perhaps it is a matter of self-pride, a threat to life or job, a family crisis, or a confrontation of some type. Alcoholics Anonymous members who have recovered through the fellowship say, "I sought help when I was sick and tired of being sick and tired." Whatever it be, there must be a reason to stop drinking.

But there is more than one way of "skinning the cat." The family, where erroneous approaches have often been used, can prompt motivation. The spouse and children certainly can and do play an important role in precipitating treatment.

Of course the key to any problem is the objective

facing of the real-life situation. There must be an elimination of denial, the eradication of the many false reasons for drinking and not seeking help. The wife, the husband, the state of society, the negative news, the boss, the changing scene, and so on, must be replaced by the reality that there exists an inability to control the intake of alcohol and that something must be done.

There are actually two methods of reaching a finale. One is the bombastic and straightforward approach, brutal and to the point, facing the abuser with the "facts of life." To do this successfully requires considerable skill.

There once was an individual who sought assistance of a certain psychiatrist. It was suggested that he visit the office prior to the appointment for a brief discussion. He refused to do so. He wanted to see the psychiatrist. The appointment was made, and the doctor in preparation for the visit, called the home to seek some additional background information.

When the client came for his appointment, he met the doctor with, "Doctor, I'm a good father, a good husband, a good provider, a good...." At that point the doctor slammed his hand on the desk and said, "You're a damn liar! You've been drunk for the past 5 years, in the hospital for the past 6 weeks, you've been out of work for the past 6 months, you beat your children, abuse your wife. You're a horrible excuse for a human being!"

The man leveled verbal abuses at the doctor, and came out seeking consolation. He was told, "You should have come by as we suggested. We would have told you if you were not going to be honest, don't go in."

Now the strange thing about it is that this person has not taken a drink in over 7 years. Each time he sees us, he says, "How is that /$!?&/ doctor?" I'm convinced that he is staying sober, attending AA, and doing other things to readjust his life, which he has done splendidly, to show that so-and-so doctor that he can do it. One cannot criticize such success.

Unless one is skilled in evaluating the situation at hand, and capable of making the brutal confrontation, one runs the risk of losing the client. And it has been said by many therapists who have long years of experience in the field of alcoholism, that if you lose the motivating experience, if you don't obtain help when it is sought, the opportunity might never present itself again. It is an awesome responsibility!

The other approach is a firm and deliberate confrontation, a type of soft-sell approach.

A certain woman came to the office and confided that her husband had been drinking too much, that he was drunk almost daily, that he had to be carried from parties and restaurants, and that he was running around with other women. To prove the latter accusation, she pointed out that he had taken his secretary out of town, and instead of going where he had said he was, took her elsewhere, and had left pictures of the trip in the camera, which he had left home, and which she had developed, not knowing what was on the roll. She wanted us to speak to her husband, whom she had thrown out of the house.

The man did come, put his right hand in the air and said, "Mister, I don't drink, I don't get drunk, I don't run around with women." At that point I said, "Look, wait a moment. If your life is so great, you really don't need me. I'm here for people who have problems. If you get along well with your wife, and you do live with your wife, don't you?"

There was a moment of mumbling, until finally he said, "Well, not, not exactly." "Well if you are living in nice surroundings, and I presume you do, don't you?" Again there was fiddling with fingers, and he finally said, "Well, not exactly." "Well, if you do live as you wish, and you don't have any problems, you really don't need me. There's no point of our chatting any further. I'm here to help people with problems. If you do have a problem one day, and would like for us to be of help, please do come. We'll be here, ready to help in any way we can."

The man departed, but two weeks later came and admitted he had a problem, and was referred to treatment.

Each method worked in the cases described. What you do, and how, depends on a number of circumstances, not least among which is the confronter's own personality and skills.

Perhaps the heavy hammer of termination can give impetus to treatment seeking. An employee who knows he or she will not be fired, "no matter what," will scarcely endeavor to solve whatever is bothering him or her.

There is really no difference in motivating the problem drinker employee than the alcoholic spouse. The spouse is not apt to change his or her way of life and drinking if no crisis, no discomfort, or no pain is encountered. Why stop if everything goes along as usual?

It is the heavy hammer of employment, the very last vestige of normal life the alcoholic wishes to discard, that often causes motivation of the client.

Termination means a crisis: a life without work; an existence without money, without food, without shelter, without an automobile, and probably without a family who must continue to exist in spite of any decision the alcoholic will make. There is no doubt about it, it is a tool much too powerful and useful to disregard.

OBJECTIVE

The objective or goal in approaching the troubled employee is to correct his or her work performance by referring him or her to diagnosis and/or treatment for whatever is amiss. Anything short of this is inadequate and useless.

Promises are worthless. How many times have alcoholics and drug abusers promised to do better! They mean to do so, and actually try everything in their power to keep their "vow." Could they or anyone else promise that cancer, pneumonia, or a virus will not occur? Ridiculous! How then can abusers guarantee a relapse will not occur?

Even *prayer* alone is often not successful. But then "God helps those who help themselves," and so without some positive action the inability to control alcohol continues.

What about *pledges?* Can you pledge immunity from sickness? Nor can the abuser pledge to anyone, even him- or herself, that the illness will disappear.

Will the fear of *hellfire* stop the abuser? If faced with the threats of hellfire for eternity, what would the drinker's reaction be? Probably stay drunk to eliminate this new problem. The drug user would stay "high" to avoid facing this new crisis. Hellfire has nothing to do with alcoholism and drug abuse. Hell is for unrepented sinners, not for sick people.

As to the imputability involved, Father John Ford is of this opinion:

> "Though the alcoholic may be powerless over alcohol and unable at times directly to resist the craving for drink, yet it is within his power generally speaking, to do something about his drinking. He is therefore responsible for taking the necessary means to get over his addiction. Most of

> them (alcoholics) undergo that process of moral deterioration for which they are in varying degrees responsible.
>
> "Objectively many alcoholics are little responsible for their condition either because their addiction has a physiological basis over which they never had control, or because, as in the case of certain primary addicts, they are compulsive drinkers almost from the beginning.
>
> "Again objectively, many other alcoholics are responsible for their condition, because it is the result of long-continued excessive drinking for which they were responsible for not having prevented it. Subjectively it seems not many alcoholics are morally guilty as far as the addiction itself is concerned."[1]

The same analogy might be drawn about drug abuse. Despite the existence of responsibility, the actual culpability of the abuser can be known to God alone, and whatever be the case, His mercy should be the motivating force, not hellfire. Avoid preaching and lecturing, a "holier-than-thou attitude," the "If you love me" appeal, threats that will not be carried out, hiding or pouring out liquor, arguing when the victim is "under the influence" or "high," making an issue over treatment, expecting an immediate recovery, and protecting the victim against alcohol or drugs.

Techniques Of Approach

The essence of the approach must be performance motivated. Moral, physical, health, family, spirituality, and other considerations, worthwhile as they may be, are secondary to the employment situation. The supervisor or employer is just that—supervisor or employer. He or she is not a social worker, physician, marriage counselor, or clergyman. The task at hand is productivity, job performance, and nothing else.

The supervisor or manager must take pains to document the performance record of the employee and be ready to verify the absence of qualtiy and quantity work or whatever other crisis or disruptive situation occurs. It is a painful task, taking away from the thrill and satisfaction of productivity, and yet it is the very essence of the technique needed to sustain and enhance production. When the final showdown occurs, and should there be arbitration, or a court battle, what is not documented will prevail little to support whatever action has been taken.

The first step after detection of a performance problem should be to discuss the matter with one's immediate superior. This will pave the way for deeper understanding, better coordination of approach, and support if needed. The confidentiality of this discussion is of paramount importance and should be scrupulously guarded.

If the suspicion of poor performance is borne out, there must be a confrontation—a face-to-face discussion with the troubled employee. This should be done on the job and on company time, for this is a business problem, a company matter, to be handled within the confines of the industrial complex, not over drinks, supper, on the patio, or over a weekend.

This is no easy task; it never is. The closer the relationship, the more difficult it can become. But a supervisor is employed and paid to be the monitor of performance, and should it wane, it is his or her responsibility to confront the employee and endeavor to rectify the situation.

In the face-to-face discussion with the employee, the supervisor should:

Be *understanding* and *fair*. The troubled employee can perceive the slightest feeling of resentment that permeates the interview or contact. There should be no exaggeration. In whatever way the supervisor would hope to be confronted in a similar situation, that should be the method used.

Be *pleasant* and *kind.* There is no room for rudeness, impoliteness, or hostility. After all, the abuser or employee is troubled, perhaps sick. Treat him or her as such, as you would like to be treated if you had a problem.

Be *sincere* in wanting to help. It is good economy and the humanitarian thing to do.

Be *firm.* Don't accept pledges, promises, and the like. Press for diagnosis and treatment, or handling of whatever is causing the problem. Don't get "sucked in" by a tear-jerking story or tale of woe. The diagnosis should come first, done so "by professionals in the medical and psychological fields who can accurately weigh all the evidence."[2]

Avoid calling or diagnosing the individual an alcoholic or addict. Let this identification be made personally or professionally. In approaching the problem, do so on a *work* or *production* basis. Endeavor to convey your interest, in terms of the person's welfare, the person's family's welfare, work, safety, and future. If the problem is admitted, the proper *referral* should be made as in any other health problem.

Don't lecture or scold. It doesn't work and never has.

Don't lose your temper with the troubled employee. Keep your cool. The person is troubled. Flying off the handle will only worsen things, enlarge whatever gap might exist between the supervisor and the client, and develop hard feelings.

If treatment is pursued, *don't expect 100% recovery*

immediately. Give the same consideration for relapse as would be given for any other illness.

Treatment must not be forced. Give the choice to the employee with the understanding, however, that the job is at stake. *Seriousness* of the problem should be explained. Work is the point in question. Should there be some request as to how performance is lagging or suffering, the supervisor should be ready with all of the appropriate *documentation,* with specifics as to absenteeism, work stoppage, slowdown of production, errors, disruptive actions, and so on. Nothing should be left unexplained.

Concern should permeate the discussion, with the supervisor accentuating the fact that he or she is interested in the employee, wishes to help the employee, has company backing to allow for assistance to be rendered in whatever way it is required. The extension of the helping hand is an essential part of the process.

After the confrontation, *a record should be made of the meeting.* Some time for readjustment should be given, and an expression of willingness to help should be followed through should a request for diagnosis or treatment ensue.

Should the employee deny any problems, or storm out, *appropriate action should be anticipated,* with a repetition of the philosophical foundation of the approach, for example, "this is a business matter, one that deals with productivity and performance, and that it is the responsibility of the worker to produce, and that of the supervisor to alert the employee when such productivity or performance is not up to standard."

After sufficient warnings, and as per the policy of the company, *disciplinary action should be taken.* Time off without pay, suspension, or whatever is outlined in company procedures should be pursued.

To avoid any stand or corrective action, regardless of the ties with the troubled employee, is nothing more or less than opening the floodgates of employment abuse.

Finally, *if the employee does not rectify or correct the performance deficiency,* at a certain point in the process, he or she must be told that it has reached a point that unless some action is taken to increase productivity, correct what is wrong, or better performance, that *termination will become necessary.* This must also be coupled with another offer to assist in alleviating whatever the problem may be, and at this point, some deadline for final action is set.

In all of the developing discussions and confrontations, it is imperative that the crucial point in question remains *performance.* At no point should the supervisor make a medical or clinical diagnosis, even though he or she is certain that the person is an alcoholic or drug abuser. That must be left to the clinician.

Most companies allow for at least two warnings, perhaps three, before considering termination, at least under ordinary circumstances. Each case must be considered and handled on its own merits. Should termination become necessary, it must be made on the basis of the employee's work performance again, and should termination occur, reconsideration for employment should be made only if treatment has been pursued.

Recognized treatment for alcoholism or drug abuse might include treatment from a physician, psychiatrist, social worker, counselor, alcoholism clinic, substance abuse center, halfway house, Alcoholics Anonymous, mental health center, or other qualified treatment resource. The therapy plan might well involve several modalities of treatment, and even several treatment centers.

SUMMARY

There is a limit to anything we can do. So it is in the case of helping troubled employees. The important thing is to realize that alcoholics and drug abusers are sick people, with peculiar personality characteristics. It is the duty of industry to detect the alcoholic and drug abuser from the point of view of safety, economics, and humanitarianism. Motivating such a person can be a difficult task. Sometimes it is impossible. Once motivated, the troubled employee must be treated by professionals in the field who are capable of coping with the many difficulties and problems. If successful in an attempt to help an employee, immeasurable good is possible for the individual and his or her family, community, church or synagogue, and the industry. On the other hand, if the unfortunate circumstances ever arise that necessitate termination, it will be comforting to realize that it was for the welfare and safety not only of the company and its many workers, but for the troubled employee as well, that the action was taken. It is possible that he or she may be motivated to seek treatment because of this jolting experience.

Troubled employees are not only treatable, but they can be productive if redirected. Rehabilitated or recovered alcoholics and drug abusers have much to contribute and can produce at a par with other workers, sometimes even more.

References

1. Ford, J.C., S.J. *Depth psychology, morality, and alcoholism.* Weston, Mass.: Weston College Press, 1951.
2. Trice, Harrison M. Identifying the problem drinker on the job. *Personnel Magazine* (American Management Association, Inc.), May 1957.

Chapter 8

CASE HISTORIES

CASE 1

John White, machinist, employed 10 years with his company. Salary $18,000 yearly. The past year he has reported tardy 10 times on Monday, and has been absent 15 Mondays. In view of his past record, little has been said about these conditions. Within the past 3 months, five jobs done on Mondays have had to be redone, causing considerable complaints from a long-time customer, and costly overtime to company in order to meet the deadlines. This has been documented and, furthermore, the supervisor informed the person next in command about the situation.

It was decided to arrange a confrontation.

White was called into the office and the supervisor opened the conversation by asking, "How are you feeling, John?"

"Fine," was the reply. "No problem."

"John," continued the supervisor, "I'm worried about you."

"What do you mean?" interjected White.

"Well, you've been with us for 10 years. And for 9 of those years, you've been a great worker. You've been so told, and the salary increments have reflected this," said the supervisor.

"I'm worried," he continued, "because I feel you are slipping. You're not producing as you should or can."

"What do you mean I'm not producing as I should or can?" said White.

"For one thing, you've been late more frequently than before," the supervisor continued.

"I told you about that," said White.

"Now wait," said the supervisor. "You said it was due to the baby's sickness. But we're talking about coming late 10 times in 6 months on Monday alone."

"What are you talking about?" said White.

"It's right here in the record," said the supervisor, pointing to the attendance book. "Furthermore, you've been absent 15 times on Monday alone during the past 6 months. Prior to that, you missed only 2 days in 9 years.

"In addition, five jobs that you did in the past half year have had to be redone, at considerable inconvenience to some good customer, plus overtime that was needed to complete the jobs that had deadlines.

"I don't know what is wrong. It's really none of my business to know. All I care about is that your performance is slipping and you are heading for trouble.

"We want to help you. We want you as a member of our production team. You're a skilled worker. You have a family, a home, and responsibilities. If something is wrong or needs attention the company wants to be of help, whatever you need. You know the company policy. Whatever you do will be kept strictly confidential."

The stage has been set.

If the worker accepts help, which in this case White did, he is sent to an appropriate facility. In this instance he was sent to a community agency and from there referred to treatment for his drinking problem, which had been the souce of his poor performance.

White's problem was a dual involvement. Marital and family pressures had reached an insurmountable point in his life. Four children had made social and financial demands which were so pressing that relief was sought through drinking. Mary, White's wife, had also become an integral part of the problem. Husband-wife relationships had deteriorated, unconsciously and inadvertently. More needed funds prompted more work; more work precipitated less time at home and with the family, less home life activities caused misunderstanding, feelings of neglect, hostility, and chaos; unresolved problems prompted more drinking and a worsening of the alcoholism problem, with the accompanying decrease in performance. Add to this the apparent inability of White to control alcohol, created a typical alcoholism case.

White and his family underwent individual and group therapy. White also joined AA, Mary, Alanon, the children, Alateen. Soon communications were reopened, drinking ceased and performance enhanced.

White kept his job, was promoted twice since, and is presently in supervision.

CASE 2

James Smith was found to be intoxicated on the job Tuesday morning. His supervisor fired him.

Smith appealed the termination. At the hearing it was brought out that Smith had exhibited numerous performance problems over a period of time, including tardiness, absenteeism, on the job drinking, mistakes, morale disturbances, intoxication on the job, and others. Further, Smith had been confronted on six various occasions and given ample opportunity of seeking help to rectify the cause of the performance problems. He had been warned that unless his performance was improved he would be terminated, and had been specifically warned about coming to work intoxicated.

In many cases today, arbiters, like courts, feel that intoxication on the job is an indication of a serious problem. In most cases the penalty is usually lessened, particularly if treatment is obtained.

On the other hand, if a worker has been frequently absent, combined misconduct with his or her drinking, did not perform as a good worker, or had refused assistance for poor performance, the termination that was precipitated by the drunkenness would probably be upheld. Such was the case with James Smith.

The termination prompted the seeking of help.

Smith's problem was crutch drinking, using alcohol to overcome his feelings of inadequacy. Drinking enabled him to communicate better, feel more comfortable. Through treatment, which included detoxification, and group therapy, Smith learned to make a realistic assessment of his skills and personality, and to use them without alcohol at an effective level.

He ultimately got another job and is presently more productive than ever before.

Case 3

Lilley went to San Francisco with his vice-president, Carlisle. During the time they were together, Lilley noticed that his friend was periodically absenting himself from the conference. He first suspected that he was going out for a drink.

Fortunately he did not accuse him of anything. He later found out that there was indeed a problem. Carlisle's wife was strung out on medication, and he was concerned about her. He called her frequently to make sure she was all right.

When an appropriate opportunity presented itself, the problem was revealed by Carlisle. Appropriate suggestion guided Carlisle to a communtiy agency capable of coping with the problem. His wife ultimately obtained help. Observation helped to redirect an otherwise very potentially destructive situation. A company program could have motivated the seeking of help.

Carlisle's wife had misued prescribed medication. Seeking numerous prescriptions from various physicians, and having been hidden by the family, she had become addicted, lost her effective role as mother and wife, and with the fear of possible overdose death, had invaded his work life. Following detoxification and a stay in an inpatient unit she returned to a normal life, allowing her husband to be capable of giving his employer full capabilities.

CASE 4

Sal worked the crane in the shipping yard as a night-shift worker. One night he dropped a ton of produce through carelessness, which missed one of the workers by only a few feet.

When his supervisor questioned him, he noticed that Sal appeared to be "drunk," or "under the influence of something." Sal was sent home because he was behaving in a rather questionable manner.

What the supervisor should have done was to send Sal to the company doctor for an examination. It is conceivable that he could have had a stroke, a slight heart attack, was sick with some illness, or have been drunk, which was the case.

Such a diagnosis can only be satisfactorily made by a physician.

In discussing the matter with the next-in-line supervisor, it was decided that the next time Sal seemed "under the weather," he would be sent to the company physician for an examination.

A month later, Sal appeared to be "under the weather." The supervisor sent him to the company doctor, who found he was intoxicated. It was later determined that he had a serious drinking problem and serious family problems.

Sal's drinking was probably the result of several factors: a possible physical inability to control drinking from the very beginning of his alcohol use (he was in trouble from the first drink); an unhappy relationship with his spouse; and the financial pressures of trying to cope with family needs.

Sal was treated, as was his family. He is now back at work, abstinent, and the life and limb of fellow workers are now protected, as is his job. This was an appropriate handling of the situation.

CASE 5

John Perry applies for a job. In the course of the interview he mentions that he had had a drinking problem, and that he had completed an inpatient session at a hospital, and was now in follow-up. Should he be considered for employment?

John is presenting for consideration his skills, not his alcoholism. If he is skilled, and is making an effort to do something about his drinking problem, then consideration should be given. If, on the other hand, he is not pursuing any treatment plan or program, the risk is increased.

The employer in this case did consider Perry's skills and the sincerity exhibited by his continued follow-up treatment and hired him.

Perry's problems were many, as is the case in most alcoholic cases. He had difficulty controlling drinking; his environment was less than acceptable, with a spouse demanding more than was humanly possible; and in-law relationships conducive to escape drinking.

During his inpatient sojourn, Perry and his wife were confronted with their interpersonal relationships. A mutual understanding resulted, enabling alcohol to become unnecessary, and preparing him anew for a happy and productive existence.

Experience has proven that with treatment and follow-up, a motivated problem drinker can be very useful and productive. Mandatory treatment as part of the process is recommended.

Case 6

Timothy Torre was a public relations officer with a certain company. Part of his duties involved entertaining customers and prospective customers. For fifteen years he lived a very hectic life, out every night with friends and customers, going to conventions, partying, all of which entailed considerable drinking.

Soon, Tim was involved in a drinking problem, and on the occasion of blackouts, forgot several appointments, including one very important one which had been made by his boss, and which triggered a confrontation.

The business lost by the missed appointment was such that serious consideration was given to terminate Tim even though he had been with the company close to 25 years, and had, up to about three years ago, been an outstanding employee.

The company in question did not have an occupational program, but the president had enough insight into the problem to seek consultation from an executive whose firm did have a program. It was pointed out that the problem seemed to have originated during the delivery of service involved in the company's business, and that since no previous confrontation and discussion had occurred that the first step should be a discussion with the employee to determine if something was indeed amiss which could be rectified.

When Tim was called into the office, the discussion focused on the missed appointments and particularly the last incidence which had cost the company considerable income. The discussion ultimately was resolved in that Tim admitted that he had a problem which was affecting his performance, and would like very much to have an opportunity to do something about it.

The president agreed and Tim was referred to a counselor who diagnosed the problem as alcoholism, which seemed to have been precipitated by continued high consumption of alcohol.

Tim went to a clinic for a number of months, accompanied by his wife, and after being detoxed on an outpatient basis, returned to work, continued to entertain customers, but now without drinking himself. For a while he had the various restaurants, lounges, and other places of entertainment which he frequented serve him his "regular," which was gingerale. No one even knew he was not drinking. Soon he cared less if anyone knew he did not drink.

Since returning to work, Tim has relanded the account which he had lost, plus maintaining the ones he was nurturing, and in addition was able to obtain several other very good accounts for his firm.

It appears that Tim's problem was a trip from heavy social drinking to alcoholic drinking. The blackout, which is a momentary period of amnesia following drinking, was a sign. If a program had been in operation, perhaps he would have been able to identify the sign with a problem and sought help before a confrontation was precipitated. Be that as it may, his recovery was complete, and shortly afterwards the company initiated a policy, supervisory training sessions to deal with such problems, an educational program with the entire work force, and a referral system to facilitate diagnosis and treatment.

CASE X

Management's view of career earning factors in heavy drinking versus moderate drinkers is a very interesting consideration. We have in most cases considered the welfare of the worker in avoiding accidents, the profits potentially available to the company or business, the family members, the community, and the worker's environment.

There is much more at stake. Human misery cannot be measured adequately. Neither can other factors that invade the alcoholic's life. But one point in question that cannot be dismissed is the monetary loss to the worker over the years, in addition to the financial loss to the company. Mr. Merle A. Gulick, vice-president of the Equitable Life Assurance Society, and past president of the National Council on Alcoholism, presented the following paper at the Conference on Alcohol and Food in Health and Disease, January 14, 1966, at the Waldorf Astoria Hotel:

A Management View Of Career Earning Factors In Heavy Drinkers Versus Moderate Drinkers

Business management, very properly, is concerned with the welfare of its employees. Salary scales and retirement benefits are merely two factors in this concern. How the employee lives on the job is also important to management. His habits are of vital concern to us...including the subject under discussion today...eating and drinking...more particularly drinking.

They are also of vital importance to the employee. They are of dollars and cents importance to him...something he may not have thought about before.

For example, at age 30, the life expectancy of a light drinker (standard risk) is 44 more years of life.

Again at age 30, the life expectancy of a heavy drinker (rated risk) is 33 more years of life.

In other words, a heavy drinker at age 30 who continues his heavy drinking habits is expected to die at age 63. The light drinker who continues to drink moderately will live to age 74, according to our company's mortality experience.

Let me explain that these are average ages. Some heavy drinkers, of course, will live beyond age 63, some will die earlier than 63. Similarly with light drinkers—some will live many years after the 74-year average and some will die before then. The ages, to repeat, reflect the average life expectancy figures.

What does this mean to the individual as translated into the economic factors of salary and retirement benefits?

It adds up to a package approximating $162,000, assuming a case history in which two men are in a given economic range. Another way of putting it might be to call it the $162,000 binge...not including the bar tab!

Let me base my figures on a hypothetical case involving two men. Larry is a light drinker and remains a light drinker all his life. Harry is a heavy drinker and remains so all his life. Each are the same age and each work for the same company. At 30, both are making $10,000 a year. At age 60, both have worked their way to annual salaries of $20,000 a year each, with parallel increments.

Now, how will the drinking habits of these two men affect the sum total of their earning capacities, all questions aside as to performance, creativity, attendance, and other job-related factors? I'm not dismissing these important elements, but since they can vary from person to person and job to job, I am looking beyond them for the purposes of discussion.

According to our figures, the heavy drinker—Harry—will die at the age of 63. Assuming that normal retirement age is 65, he will work two years less than Larry, the light drinker. That means, first, that the light drinker will earn $40,000 more in salary, remembering that both men had reached the $20,000-a-year bracket at age 60.

The heavy drinker thus will be denied at least two years of salary, since he will have died at 63.

Furthermore, he will be denied nine additional years of normal retirement benefits that Larry, the light drinker, will enjoy since Larry will be alive during this period according to our mortality tables.

This retirement benefit comes to a pretty package, varying from company to company, of course. At Equitable, which is fairly representative of the industry, a salaried employee who makes $10,000 at age 30 and works his way up to an annual salary of $20,000 a year at age 60 can expect to retire at 65 with a retirement benefit—in round—of $11,200 a year based on our most recent retirement figures. Add to this social security payments of about $200 a month for himself and his wife, and the figure comes to a tidy $13,600 a year.

Now, to get the total economic impact, multiply this figure by the number of retirement years that Larry, the light drinker, will enjoy—nine beyond the retirement age of 65 until he reaches his standard mortality age of 74—and you get $122,400 in all.

That's exactly $122,400 that Harry, the heavy drinker, will never see. Because Harry will have been dead all these years.

A bit more arithmetic and we can complete the picture.

Add the two years of salary of $40,000 that Larry made to his retirement benefits, and we get a total approximately $162,000...as against nothing for Harry, the heavy drinker—if his happens to be a noncontributory plan. Now I'm not including insurance and other death benefits or savings or any other personal factors that might be involved.

Even so, limiting myself to the economic factors of salary and retirement benefits alone, the light drinker comes out $162,000 ahead of the heavy drinker...plus 11 more years of added life, with all its concomitant joys and sorrows.

$162,000...some binge!

Talk given by Merle A. Gulick, Vice-President, The Equitable Life Assurance Society, at the Conference on Alcohol and Food in Health and Disease, January 14, 1966, at the Waldorf Astoria Hotel.

Chapter 9

COMPANY EDUCATIONAL PROJECTS

Management and supervision are only two phases of a company structure. For an occupational program to be truly viable, there has to be total participation and involvement: management, labor, and the entire work-force.

To facilitate the acceptance and implementation of company policy and procedure, the prompting of early detection of employee and employee family problems, the seeking of appropriate diagnosis and treatment, and hopefully the prevention of alcohol, drugs, and related problems, a comprehensive plan can be developed.

SAFETY DEPARTMENT

Since the main objective of the safety department is to promote safety, both on and off the job, the topics related to alcohol and drugs are most pertinent.

There should be no objection to the inclusion of alcohol and drugs as part of the safety department's program in view of these facts:

--Fifty percent (50%) of transportational fatalities have incidence of alcohol.
--Seventy percent (70%) of one-driver one-car fatality, the driver was drunk.
--Forty-nine percent (49%) of suicide victims were drinking at time of death.
--Sixty percent (60%) of all injuries have incidence of alcohol.
--Seventy percent (70%) of all homicides have alcohol or drugs involved.
--Thirty-three percent (33%) of all suicides are alcoholics.
--Fifty percent (50%) of all rapes have the incidence of alcohol.

Some possible topics for consideration are:

Alcohol—the physiology and behavioral aspects of alcohol as it pertains to safety at work, home, and play. Tips for safe drinking.
Drugs—effects of drugs on behavior and skills, with a review of the types, classifications, dangers, and the like.
Attitudes and emotions—how they affect skills and dangers of negativism.
Driving—defensive driving and effects of alcohol on driving skills.
Films—dealing with safety in general, home safety concerns, driving, and so on.

The possibilities are endless. Safety is everyone's business. If it is neglected and tragedy occurs, everyone suffers: the individual, the family, the company, and the community.

GENERAL EMPLOYEE GROUP

Everyone must be made part of the company program and the following might well be considered as possible topics for discussion:

Safety aspects of alcohol—physiology and behavioral aspects as they relate to work, home, and play.

Alcoholism—defined and explained, with emphasis on its early detection, its treatability , and its prevention.

Drugs—use, abuse, effects, identification, prevention, and treatment.

Handling personal and family problems—a review of alternatives.

Community resources—review of available resources for alcohol, drug, family, health, mental health, and other problems.

Company policy—a review of company policy dealing with problem employees and approved procedures of action.

Films—dealing with safety, alcohol, family relationships, drugs, and so forth.

If we acknowledge that it is impossible to divorce personal and family problems from the office or plant, at least for any significant period of time, then the number of program topics for the general work force is endless.

Supervisory Force

While some of the possible topics have already been reviewed, the following might serve as a guide for supervisory training planning:

Role of the supervisor—including responsibilities.
Alcohol and alcoholism—understanding the safety aspects of alcohol and the etiology of alcoholism as it affects the work force and production.
Drugs—identification, detection, and understanding effects.
Documentation—review of need and technique of documentation of performance.
Confrontation—the do's and don't's of confrontation.
Understanding people—to supervise and help them better and to prompt the enhancement of performance.
Company policy and procedures—review of the company's policy and implementation procedures.
Community resources—availability of resources for the troubled employee.
Films—dealing with supervision, alcohol, handling of people, confrontation, and so on.

Films

There are catalogues available with details of purchase and rental rates of 16-mm films appropriate for occupational and general use. Following is a list with brief description of some of these films:

Need for Decision
Produced by Union Carbide
Peckham Productions
9 East 48th Street
New York, New York 10017
(Supervisor identifies employee with a performance problem that is alcohol related. An approach is made.)

Dryden File
Motivision, Ltd/Newsfilm U.S.A.
21 West 46th Street
New York, New York 10036
(Company program is finally ulitilized after needless manipulation by problem drinker, and results of manager to admit need for help.)

Case 7201
International Producer Services
3518 Cahuenga Blvd. West
Hollywood, California 90068
(Deals with woman alcoholic.)

The Distant Drummer series
NIMH
5600 Fishers Lane
Rockville, Maryland 20852
(Drug film.)

Training Program
American Hospital Association

Multi-Media Training Program
Helen McGuire
Director of Professional Services
American Hospital Association
840 Lake Shore Drive
Chicago, Illinois 60611

99 Bottles of Beer
Norm Southerby & Associates
P.O. Box 15403
Long Beach, California 90815
(Alcohol abuse film aimed at young people.)

Secret Love of Sandra Blaine
Norm Southerby & Associates
P.O. Box 15403
Long Beach, California 90815
(Story of woman alcoholic and how she destroys her family—road to recovery.)

Alcoholism in Industry
Filmstrip—sound
National Institute for Occupational Safety and Health
1014 Broadway
Cincinnati, Ohio 45202
(Business and industry personnel material.)

DWI-Phoenix
Local American Automobile Association Clubs
AAA Foundation for Traffic Safety
734 Fifteenth Street, N.W.
Washington, D.C. 20005

A Firm Hand
Marketing Director
Addiction Research Foundation
33 Russell Street
Toronto, Canada M5S2S1
(Job performance situations.)

Problems vs Profits
Texas Commission on Alcoholism
809 Sam Houston State Office Building
Austin, Texas 78701
(Overview of occupational alcohol abuse and alcoholism.)

A Snort History
Denver Alcohol Safety Action Project
1845 Sherman Street
Denver, Colorado 80203
(Clever cartoon and live action film on drinking and driving.)

To Your Health
Center for Mass Communication
Columbia University Press
136 South Broadway
Irvington, New York 10533
(Informational film about alcohol, attitudes, alcoholism, and treatment.)

Reds, Whites, and Booze
Lynnville Metropolitan Office
230 Oak Grove
Minneapolis, Minnesota 55403
(Family life in our drug-comfort-oriented society.)

The Drug Scene
Hanna-Barbera Productions
Aims
P.O. Box 1010
Hollywood, California 90028

Narcotics—The Inside Story
Aims
P.O. Box 1010
Hollywood, California 90028

Post Mortem
Aims

P.O. Box 1010
Hollywood, California 90028

PAYROLL INSERTS

Another method of penetrating the work force with the message of the company's program and the realities of drinking and alcoholism, is to utilize the payroll envelope. Specially devised inserts can be very helpful particularly within the family setting. It often prompts action without the involvement of industry itself.

Examples of several inserts utilized in the New Orleans area are the following:

HAPPINESS IS...

A home and family free from the problems of alcoholism and drug abuse.

For FREE and CONFIDENTIAL information call **524-HELP**

Your Committee on ALCOHOLISM and DRUG ABUSE
for Greater New Orleans • A United Fund Agency

If you have a drinking problem . . . contact: COMMITTEE ON ALCOHOLISM — 524-HELP
(A United Fund Agency)

HAPPY PAY DAY

HAPPINESS IS....
a Home and Family free from the problems of alcoholism and drug abuse.

For FREE and CONFIDENTIAL INFORMATION call

524-HELP

Your Committee on Alcoholism and Drug Abuse
for Greater New Orleans
A United Fund Agency

MATERIALS

Outlined and developed talks on alcohol and drugs as well as some visual aids are available from the Committee on Alcoholism & Drug Abuse for Greater New Orleans, 3314 Conti Street, New Orleans, Louisiana 70119.

SUMMARY

Audiovisual aids add zest to programs. In addition, because it involves additional senses, the potential for retention is much greater.

For a company program to reap full harvest, every employee should in some way be exposed not only to the pertinent ingredients of the approved policy and procedures, but to general facts as well. Alcohol and drugs permeate our culture. The risk of personal and/or family exposure and involvement is high. Knowing what, why, and how to handle such problems as they occur is important.

Chapter 10

REFERRAL

GENERAL NEEDS

Detection of the troubled worker is only the first step in the salvage process. Assistance, geared to the needs of the individual, must be available.

Alcoholism, being such a complex problem, necessitates referral to cover the following categories:

Acutely ill and intoxicated alcoholics and drug abusers.

Nonacutely intoxicated alcoholics and drug abusers.

Sober alcoholics and "clean" drug abusers.

Families of alcoholics and drug abusers.

Acutely ill and intoxicated alcoholics and drug abusers require medical attention. This need must be met by physicians willing to treat such clients and even make house calls. Detoxification centers, hospital beds, and emergency room services are only some of the ways medical emergencies must be handled. Without these services life and rehabilitation possibilities can be lost.

Nonacutely intoxicated alcoholics and drug abusers usually do not represent medical emergencies. They are indeed in crisis, and there is a need for, at the least, a form of crisis intervention since they represent a form of psychiatric emergency. AA offers a 24-hour 12-Step Call Program for alcoholics who wish to talk to someone and who wish to be helped. There are groups in almost every town. Crisis centers, hotlines, mental health centers, mental health associations, alcoholism clinics, drug abuse clinics, substance abuse centers, alcoholism information centers, doctors, psychiatrists, and others are excellent avenues of handling such problems.

Sober alcoholics and "clean" drug abusers who present themselves sober and drug free and who wish to remain so and wish to redirect and readjust their lives present the greatest challenge. They may need one or more of a host of services: evaluation, medical care, psychological aid, psychiatric help, Alcoholics Anonymous, food, employment, shelter, vocational rehabilitation, training, spiritual counseling, marriage counseling, and so on.

The family of problem drinkers and drug abusers also need comfort, psychological support, psychiatric help, emergency food, shelter, legal aid, and counseling.

Such a variety of resources requires considerable planning on the part of an industry. In addition, a team approach must be developed if significant success is to be attained. Problems of any sort affect the entire person: body, mind, and soul. No single therapist can hope to treat all problem employees with any appreciable degree of success.

If there is a Council or Committee on Alcoholism or

Drug Abuse in the area, or an N.C.A. affiliate, it would be wise to contact the agency before developing any referral list.

THE MEDICAL PROFESSION

The alcoholic and drug abusers, because they are sick, should be primarily referred to the medical profession. Where possible, the medical department of the company should be involved so proper diagnosis can be made. Where businesses or plants are not adequately staffed medically, outside assistance must be obtained.

The medical profession is an integral part of the treatment team. If the alcoholic or drug abuser is indeed sick, he or she belongs in the capable hands of a physician. In some isolated cases the physician will be the only therapist needed. For others, his or her services will either be the beginning of treatment or not be necessary at all. But in all cases, the physician should make a thorough diagnosis to assure physical comfort on the part of the patient, and to further assure rational drug freeness without which treatment would be impossible.

Despite the fact that most alcoholics and drug users are not psychotic or neurotic, the services of a psychiatrist should be available for at least diagnostic or evaluative purposes. Since most troubled employees suffer from emotional problems, the role of the psychiatrist in the overall team approach cannot be overemphasized. In some instances, psychiatric therapy will be required.

Where annual physicals are mandatory, some questioning on the amount and frequency of drinking and other drug usage should be included. This is not to indicate or insinuate that there exists suspicions that alcoholism or drug abuse might be rampant in the company, but rather to serve as a means of diagnosing early cases of abuse, to allow such problems to become a more respectable part of the plant's medical vocabulary, and to permit physician-to-client discussion.

Industrial nurses who are alert can contribute to detection and alleviation of problem drinking and drug abuse. They usually witness early manifestations of trouble.

Counselors And Social Workers

During the development of personal or family problems, the employee loses friends and destroys family communications. On the outside he or she is shunned and avoided as a nuisance and plague; on the inside he or she is misunderstood, and the family role shaken or destroyed.

Friendships must be rebuilt and others eliminated. New friends, capable of assisting in the maintenance of sobriety and drug-free living, must be sought. This requires professional help; seldom can a person do it alone.

If alcoholism and drug abuse have progressed to any degree, there will undoubtedly exist in the home—if it is still together—a complete lack of communication. It is very difficult for one spouse to exhibit love and affection to the other spouse who comes home nightly in an inebriated condition or "stoned" on drugs. In addition to the deterioration of husband-wife relationships, the children become seriously affected. They yearn to escape from their disturbing surroundings, from an atmosphere of confusion and chaos, and from an environment where they cannot invite their friends for fear of being humiliated or embarrassed. Without proper guidance, they will leave home early, marry the wrong partner through motivation of escape rather than love, and embark on another generation of misery.

The counselor or social worker is needed to put these family and social areas in good functioning order. Families must be brought together through group therapy or other means. It may be necessary to have the husband and wife, or husband, wife, and children together. Whatever be the technique used, again a professional is needed.

Too frequently, the family of the troubled employee is neglected. There are times when the spouse or family member may be in more dire need of therapy than the sick employee. A nagging, demanding, selfish spouse can aggravate the problem and prevent treatment or permanent recovery. Here, again, the counselor or social worker will be capable of rendering the advice or therapy needed to "clear the air."

The family plays an integral part in the treatment process. Regardless of who may require more direction or counseling, the abuser or the spouse, recovery and developing a new life-style will come only when family members unite in a common cause.

THE CLERGY

The contribution that the clergy can make to rehabilitation is not to be underestimated. Many people seek advice and help from their clergy before speaking to anyone. This is particularly true in alcohol and drug problems. Humans have a spiritual component. This component suffers like all the other areas of life as substance abuse develops. Ultimately, if the abuser is to enjoy permanent success in coping with his or her problem, spiritual readjustment and serenity are needed.

Inpatient Services

When the progressiveness of the addiction has reached the point that outpatient treatment is not sufficient, inpatient care may be required—getting away from the environment in a retreat setting where in-depth therapy is administered, an evaluation of one's total life is made, and a plan of action formulated.

Some halfway houses can usually afford this form of assistance. Others have a "work out and sleep in" program coupled with therapy to help the abuser.

There are *long- and short-term treatment centers* located in hospitals, mental health centers, mental hospitals, and special facilities in private and government-funded facilities.

A number of *private hospitals and treatment centers* are available for clients who wish to seek help out-of-town or who wish to take advantage of the experience that some of these facilities have amassed over the years. Information concerning these resources can be obtained from local councils, clinics, or from national organizations.

Alcoholics Anonymous

Perhaps the most successful treatment program for alcoholics is Alcoholics Anonymous or AA. AA is a fellowship of men and women who have a common problem —they are all alcoholics. They support each other in their sobriety, by a simple 12-step program. Members attend meetings on an anonymous basis, using only first names to protect the identity of the alcoholic. *Open meetings* can be attended by anyone and are open to the public. *Closed meetings* are for alcoholics only. Membership is open to any alcoholic who wishes to overcome alcoholism. There are no dues.

AA was founded in 1934 by Doctor Bob and Will W., two alcoholics who had, up to that time, been hopelessly caught up in the throes of alcoholism. The group they developed has grown until today it has chapters in all parts of the world.

The 12 steps of Alcoholics Anonymous are:

Step 1 — "We admitted we were powerless over alcohol—that our lives had become unmanageable."

Step 2 — "Came to believe that a Power greater than ourselves could restore us to sanity."

Step 3 — "Made a decision to turn our will and our lives over to the care of God as we understood Him."

Step 4 — "Made a searching and fearless moral inventory of ourselves."

Step 5 — "Admitted to God, to ourselves, and to another human being, the exact nature of our wrongs."

Step 6 — "Were entirely ready to have God remove all these defects of character."

Step 7 — "Humbly asked Him to remove our shortcomings."

Step 8 — "Made a list of all persons we had harmed, and became willing to make amends to them all."

Step 9 — "Made amends to such people wherever possible, except when to do so would injure them or others."

Step 10 — "Continued to take personal inventory and when we were wrong promptly admitted it."

Step 11 — "Sought through prayer and meditation to improve our conscious contact with God as we understood Him, praying only for knowledge of His will for us and the power to carry that out."

Step 12 — "Having had a spiritual awakening as the result of these steps, we tried to carry this message to alcoholics, and to practice these principles in all our affairs."

An in-depth review of the program indicates that successful adherence to the 12 steps will promote much more than sobriety. It is a program of perfection.

Alcoholics Anonymous members endeavor to maintain sobriety, one day at a time, which accumulates into days, weeks, months, and years if successfully pursued. The key is surrender, honesty, and giving the program to others, which is done on a one-to-one basis, through the 12-step call where an alcoholic calls on another alcoholic who is in trouble and who is seeking help.

Meetings are much like nonprofessional group therapy sessions where alcoholics take hope and courage in seeing what others have done and making sobriety also a part of their own lives.

AA is deeply spiritual, although it is no religion, nor is it associated with any religious group or denomination. The program relies on God or "a higher power" as He is seen by individual members and this characteristic has contributed significantly to its success.

To belong to AA one must be an alcoholic and be willing to do something about his or her drinking problem. The anonymity of the member is maintained, and to this purpose, only first names are used.

Closed meetings of AA are reserved for alcoholics only; open meetings can be attended by both alcoholics and nonalcoholics. In both instances, the alcoholics who discuss their problems and recovery give only their first name.

Alanon is a sister group of AA. It is for the wife, husband, family member, and friend of the alcoholic. It also utilizes meetings on an anonymous basis and helps the family member or friend to learn how to live with the problem. Alanon members also make themselves available to discuss alcoholism with other people in trouble.

While the main purpose of Alanon is to help family members live with the problem in a sane manner, there are times that what is learned from Alanon is very helpful in not only maintaining the serenity of the family, but in prompting action on the part of the alcoholic. As in the case of AA, Alanon members maintain their anonymity.

Alateen is for the children of alcoholics, who need to understand the disease concept of the problem and to interpret appropriately the manifestations of the illness. The meetings are held on an anonymous basis also. We strongly urge the utilization of AA, Alanon, and Alateen.

SUMMARY

The help of the company medical department, the employee assistance counselor, if there is one, and community resources are needed to help in the recovery process. Care must be taken to assure meaningful follow-up.

Clients who express a desire to be assisted must exhibit determination to pursue some form of treatment. Few problem drinkers or drug abusers can cope effectively with their problem without help. It is also a sign of willingness to do something constructively to redirect one's life-style and work performance.

It is also recommended that in approaching a troubled employee that every effort be exerted to maintain communication with one's immediate supervisor and seek advice from qualified agencies or individuals.

A dual referral is again urged—help from clinic resources and AA.

Chapter 11

RESOURCES

Industry personnel have at their disposal numerous resources of information regarding alcoholism and drug abuse. Many may be found in the yellow pages of the local telephone directory. Listed below are some of the more common agencies that will provide needed information related to alcohol and drugs.

LOCAL

Alanon
Alateen
Alcoholics Anonymous
Alcoholism clinics
Clergy
Councils on alcoholism
Crisis intervention centers
Detoxification centers
Doctors and psychiatrists
Drug abuse councils
General and private hospitals
Halfway houses
Health departments
Mental health centers
Narcotics anonymous
Police and sheriffs departments

Private counseling centers
Recovery, Inc.
Referral centers
Sheltered workshops
Suicide prevention centers
Welfare departments

State

Law Enforcement Agency (Justice Department)
State Alcoholism Authority
State Drug Abuse Authority
Veterans Administration hospitals

National

Alcohol and Drug Problems Association of North America
1101 Fifteenth Street, N.W.
Washington, D.C. 20036

American Medical Association
535 N. Dearborn Street
Chicago, Illinois 60610

American Nurses' Association
2420 Pershing Road
Kansas City, Missouri 64108

American Public Health Association
1015 Eighteenth Street, N.W.
Washington, D.C. 20036

American Personnel and Guidance Association
1607 New Hampshire Avenue, N.W.
Washington, D.C. 20009

American Psychological Association
1200 Seventh Street, N.W.
Washington, D.C. 20037

Narcotics Addiction Rehabilitation Branch

Division of Narcotic Addiction and Drug Abuse
National Institute of Mental Health
5600 Fishers Lane
Rockville, Maryland 20852

National Council on Alcoholism
733 Third Avenue
New York, New York 10017

National Institute on Alcohol Abuse and Alcoholism
5600 Fishers Lane
Rockville, Maryland 20852

National Institute on Drug Abuse
5600 Fishers Lane
Rockville, Maryland 20852

National Institute of Mental Health
5600 Fishers Lane
Rockville, Maryland 20852

Office of Scientific Support
U.S. Department of Justice Drug Enforcement Administration
1405 I Street, N.W.
Washington, D.C. 20537

Veterans Rehabilitation
Alcohol and Drug Dependence Service
Department of Medicine and Surgery
Veterans Administration
Washington, D.C. 20420

Chapter 12

IN CONCLUSION

THE WASTEFUL HANGOVER

America is a land of "plenty." Amid the prosperity lies a culture of leisure, status seeking, and drinking. We meet our friends over drinks, greet our business associates with cocktails, enjoy our food with "before" and "after" alcoholic beverages, celebrate anniversaries and special events with toasts, and interpret sociability, comradeship, and fun with imbibing. The fun, togetherness, and business atmosphere usually associated with drinking are unfortunately shrouded by the by-products of pathological and irresponsible drinking.

There is an alarmingly increased number of drinkers who intentionally, unintentionally, unconsciously, or through ignorance do not care to drink responsibly and safely. They contribute significantly to the American Hangover, as do those drinkers who, because of an insidious illness, are unable to drink socially, moderately, and controllably.

Two-thirds of Americans are classified as "social drinkers," and for the most part are never adversely affected by their drinking habits. How many drink abusively is difficult to ascertain. However, a small percentage do become involved in problem drinking. In fact, I of every 15 drinkers for one reason or another eventually develops the illness of alcoholism, and this apparently small minority is conservatively calculated to be a staggering nine and a half million!

Despite the belief to the contrary, most alcoholics come from the middle and upper strata of society. They are men and women who have families, own homes, automobiles, have jobs, church and synagogue affiliations, and typical everyday responsibilities. Ninety-seven percent of alcoholics come from this segment of the population, while only three percent can be found on Skid Row.

Alcoholism is increasing at an alarming rate. It is our nation's most serious major public health problem and if all the facts were authentically recorded and interpreted, probably our number one killer.

Injury And Death

While it is difficult to ascertain the exact extent alcoholism per se contributes to accidents, injuries, and fatalities, some startling figures do reveal the contribution of alcohol misuse to safety hazards:

Over fifty percent (50%) of transportational accidents involve drinking.

Seventy percent (70%) of one-car transportational fatalities, the driver had been drinking.

Sixty percent (60%) of all injuries have incidence of drinking.

According to a recent publication by Allstate Insurance, one (1) of every fifty (50) drivers you meet on the highway is drunk!

Social Problems

According to the latest data available:

One half (50%) of all homicides, the victim or the one who committed the crime, or both, had been drinking.

A drinking problem could be traced to fifty percent (50%) of all broken families, separations, or divorces.

One-third of all suicides in our country were alcoholics last year.

Forty-nine percent (49%) of all suicide victims were drinking at the time of their death.

A significant percentage of delinquency cases have a history of a family drinking problem.

A significant percentage of marital problems, many easily acknowledged, others which find their way into courts, have drinking involved.

The Law

Furthermore, it is estimated that:

A significant number of felony offenses are committed under the influence of alcohol.

According to a New Mexico study, 50% of rapes have an incidence of alcohol.

Most disturbances of the peace involve drinking.

Until recently, the alcoholic was generally classified, along with the drunk, as a municipal offender. He or she was, and to some extent still is, hunted down, picked up, brought before the court, and jailed. This complex procedure is costly. There is the financial burden of keeping policemen on the streets, the pickup vehicles, the expense of valuable time, booking the "offender," the trial, and usually more transportation to jail, plus the cost of incarceration.

Medical Costs

The many physical and psychological complications of alcoholism are further absorbed in dollars and cents by the American public. Over $50,000,000 are spent each year for the care of alcoholics in state institutions. The cost to individual alcoholics (including their insurance policies), who are hospitalized under many and varied diagnoses, would probably run into astronomical figures. Some mental hospitals have estimated that between 80% and 90% of the first admissions to their institutions have been alcoholics.

Industrial Cost

Placing a dollar sign on the loss sustained by an industry through the employee troubled with alcoholism would be impossible. There are figures that are quoted, but even the $10.4 billions could be conservative. It is a problem that can drain a company of the cream of production and profit.

Human Misery

Even the cost of welfare organizations for the care of alcoholics and their families are overshadowed by the human misery of the victim and his or her environment. The alcoholic finds himself eventually alone, without work, family, money, shelter, hopes, goals—everything that all of us consider synonymous with life.

The family squabbles, wrecked lives, financial heartaches, broken families, divorces, and physical punishment associated with alcoholism, cannot be calculated in dollars and cents. Alcoholism is truly "the illness everyone hates, but few understand." The last step along the road of alcoholism is faulty health, malnutrition, liver damage, brain damage, and Skid Row.

Conclusion

Alcoholism can strike anyone: executive, housewife, doctor, lawyer, school teacher, nurse, skilled or unskilled laborer, even the clergy. There is no shame in the affliction; it is an illness, albeit a costly one. If there is a shameful aspect of alcoholism it is that its victims do not come forth earlier to seek treatment.

If you have ever suffered a "blackout"—which is a period of amnesia following drinking; if you need drinks to calm your nerves; if you miss work because of drinking; if you use alcohol as a crutch; if you suffer tremors or shakes because of your drinking; if you go on benders; if you drink eye openers; if your life is disturbed in any way because of drinking; if your family life suffers because of your alcohol consumption; or if you cannot control your drinking—you owe it to yourself and to your family to seek help.

Left untreated, alcoholism will continue to progress

and rob you of health and prosperity. Treated, it can be arrested, and its victim returned to normal and productive living.

For those who can drink, drinking can be fun, socially lubricating, and, if indulged in safely and moderately, will cause no harm. Unrestrained and irresponsible drinking can cause loss of limb and life. Alcoholism destroys completely—emotionally, physically, financially, socially, and spiritually!

Should alcoholism or drug abuse strike in the confines of your family, remember it is an illness; if it is present in your business—and if you are immune, you are the exception—you owe it to your business and to your employees to endeavor to end the costly hangover.

INDEX

CONCILIUM

Religion in the Seventies

Concilium 113 (3/1978): Dogma